I0471739

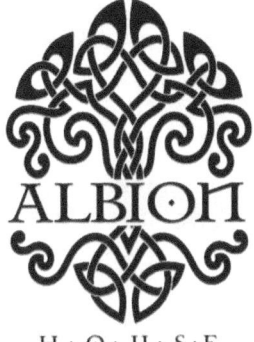

Albion House Publishing

Cover design, interior design and all illustration work by
John W Henson unless otherwise stated. Final preparation
for press by Albion House

ISBN: 978-1-291-92499-2

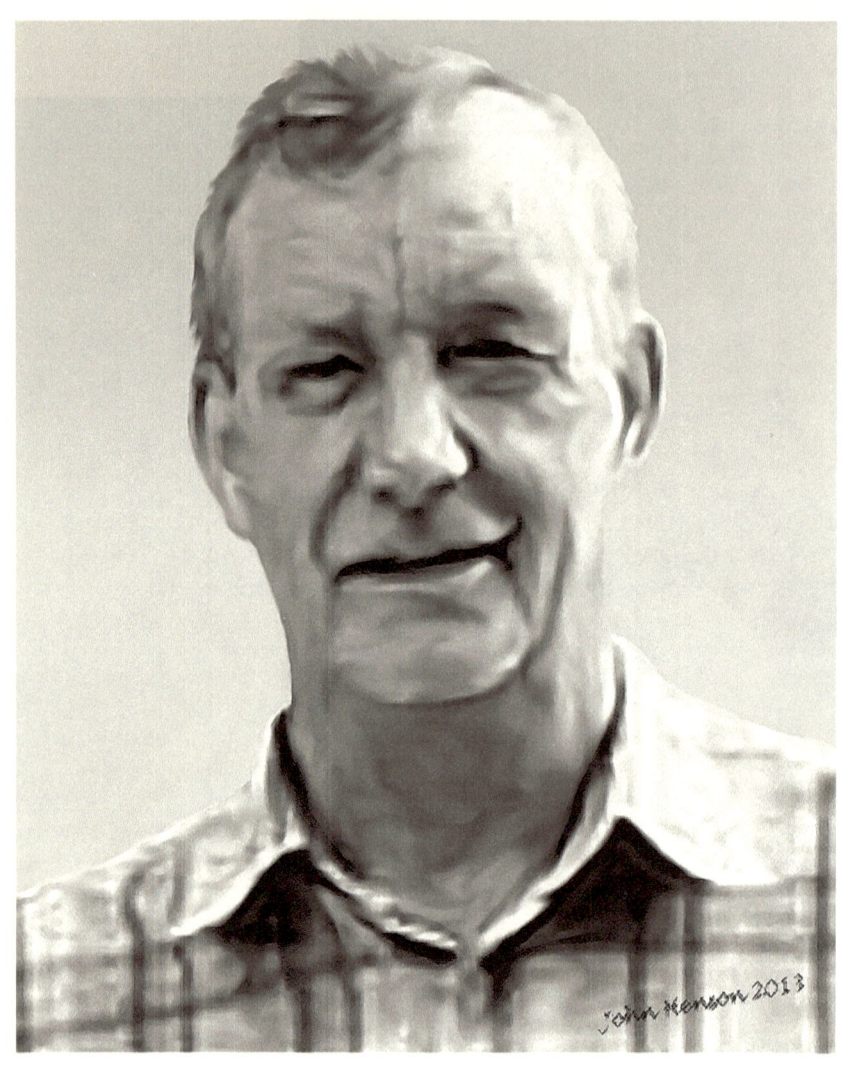

This book is dedicated to the memory of
Roger Anthony Cope Scothern. My teacher, my mentor
my friend........ 1944-2011

Acknowledgements

To Mr. Roger Anthony Cope Scothern my teacher and friend for teaching me about art and faith

Thank you Sir!

To Peter Parr my tutor at art college for teaching me to draw from life

Thank you!

To my daughter Ruth Elizabeth Henson for inspiring me in more ways than she will ever know

Thank you!

To my friend Paulette for inspiring the Chronicles of Gildas and giving me the chance to illustrate 'The Tale of Kathleen Laoghaire

Thank you!

To all of the numerous family and friends that have Commissioned or inspired or otherwise added to my portfolio over the years

Thank you!

Foreword

Graphite Lines is a moving tribute to John's teacher, mentor and friend Roger Anthony Cope Scothern. It is a graphic journal that superbly illustrates John Henson's lifelong love of art in all its forms. It is a fitting tribute to a mentor who ignited the artist's talent in ways he could never have imagined. It is a triumph all teachers hope to achieve, to motivate their students to their own greatness, to create from the passion of their own visions!

Thus you will see within the covers of this book, John's inspired drawings. Drawings that will take you through the ages, revealing beautifully drawn portraits that penetrate the soul and show you the whimsy and joy that resides within this exceptional man. John has a gift for capturing emotion with his brilliant pencil that I have rarely seen.

Personally, I'm privileged that he agreed to illustrate my epic poem, The Tale of Kathleen Laoghaire. I will be forever grateful for the deeply insightful art he contributed to my piece.

So please enjoy the breathtaking Graphite Lines! John has compiled this book to honor the memory of his mentor and friend! So powerful are the words and artistic expressions of John Henson, one cannot view his works and not be deeply moved.

It is my honor and pleasure to write this foreword. I invite you to plunge into the extraordinary, enchanted world of John W. Henson and discover his magic for yourselves!

P. F. Kosak, Novelist/Poet

Authors Introduction

I have been drawing since I could hold a pencil
I recall the heady days of my childhood, and even
back then, to me all my drawings had a life and in
those early formative years they came with sound
effects. Like all small boys my drawings of battles
had explosions and gunfire and as I matured music
But the adults laughed. To me the drawings had a
reality and they still do. You see I learned that what
I could not articulate with words, my pictures were
Very eloquent in. One man understood this Mr Roger
Anthony Cope Scothern my art teacher at 'Welbeck
Road School for Boys' and I owe to him what I can
do today He laid the foundation for the ability that
could show what I had in my minds eye and could
record those images that I had created in my head
and the ones that I saw outside and give pleasure
to others by doing so. I found that others had their
images that they were not lucky enough to have the
ability to record so I did it for them and commissions
started to come in. Since then I have attended
university and gained qualifications to degree level
and travelled the world but the joy and wonder never
left me. I still see magic in everything and am always
amazed at what I do, I am and have been a very lucky
man This book is just a few examples of what I have
done in recent years from commission work to cartoons
for my children and various nephews and nieces. It's
more than half a century now since that little lad picked
up his first pencil and discovered and is still discovering
the beauty and the power of 'Graphite Lines'.

Thank you Sir

A gentle man, with a kind heart
Long hair and a baggy pullover
Your appearance set you apart
When others failed you took over

Words that should have been
Spoken in my father's voice
Never came, caring unseen
To this little boy you gave a choice

You taught me art and religion too
Laying the foundations of my life
These things would see me through
All the pain, the trouble and strife

My teacher, my mentor, my friend
That made me what I am today
Making sure my talent did not end
When others would have taken it away

Sadly now you are gone from here
You'll always stand out from the crowd
A man and a teacher without peer
I hope that I would have made you proud

I never had chance to tell you what you meant
To say thank you Sir just for being there
For you were a gift Heaven sent
To a little boy with no one to care

For Mr Roger Anthony Cope Scothern 1944-2011.
My Teacher, my mentor, my friend

Beauty in Graphite Lines

I construct the lines that become your face
As the light and shade create surface form
Weight of line the distance begins to trace
Fading shadows making the features warm

Faint lines reflect the dimness of days gone by
A lonely child hiding from all behind the mask
Growing within her world as stronger tones vie
An inquisitive child who is never afraid to ask

Moving forward the strong lines give power
A beautiful woman of character will now look
Through her eyes a Princess in her ivory tower
Strokes make you stand forth in my sketchbook

In graphite lines I create the reality of the images
Tracing the history and emotions of love and tears
Things of beauty created on woven white pages
Time flowing, shaded image, telling the tale of years

In my hands I have the gift of creating great beauty
The ability to record nature's most stunning designs
For this I consider it to be my God given duty
To set down these things by the power in graphite lines

Light and shade will add subtlety to your character
Giving depth and volume to the image in this place
From my mind and heart this graphite vision I transfer
As I tell the story of the life hidden in a beautiful face

Welbeck Road School for Boys

Welbeck Road you were our school
A bastion of great reputation
A place where we broke every rule
As you tried to give us an education

We learned our lessons from the best
They taught us without reservation
To make us achieve ahead of the rest
They deserved a standing ovation

They taught us English, and Maths, Sciences too
History, Geography, Music and Art
School plays and operas we performed quite a few
Our talented teachers also took part

Topsy Turvey's trouble with his bacon slicer
The herald of every music lesson's beginning
Edison Jones lessons couldn't have been nicer
His miscounted cane strokes were winning

Mr Scothern our Art teacher knew
That Lenny and John had a talent
For skiving and painting scenery too
The love of Academia not apparent

Mr Stanton with his board rubber threw
To where every pupils head was at
Without even looking, somehow he knew
And we always wondered, how does he do that

Mr Picard with Science tried to enlighten us
We blew up his classroom with magnesium foil
We put it in water, what was the fuss
No one had said that dirty water was oil

English was Peter Parker, Spiderman no less
Mrs Gee tried to teach us History
We were a motley crew, I must confess
How they taught us at all is a mystery.

We learned Woodwork and metalwork too
The latter was taught by Mr Pig
Meda, meda bald header, Mr Medley to you
The school hierarchies Mr Big

But the good old days do not last
We no longer hear the playground's noise
Just a ghost in our schoolboy past
Where once stood Welbeck Road School for Boys

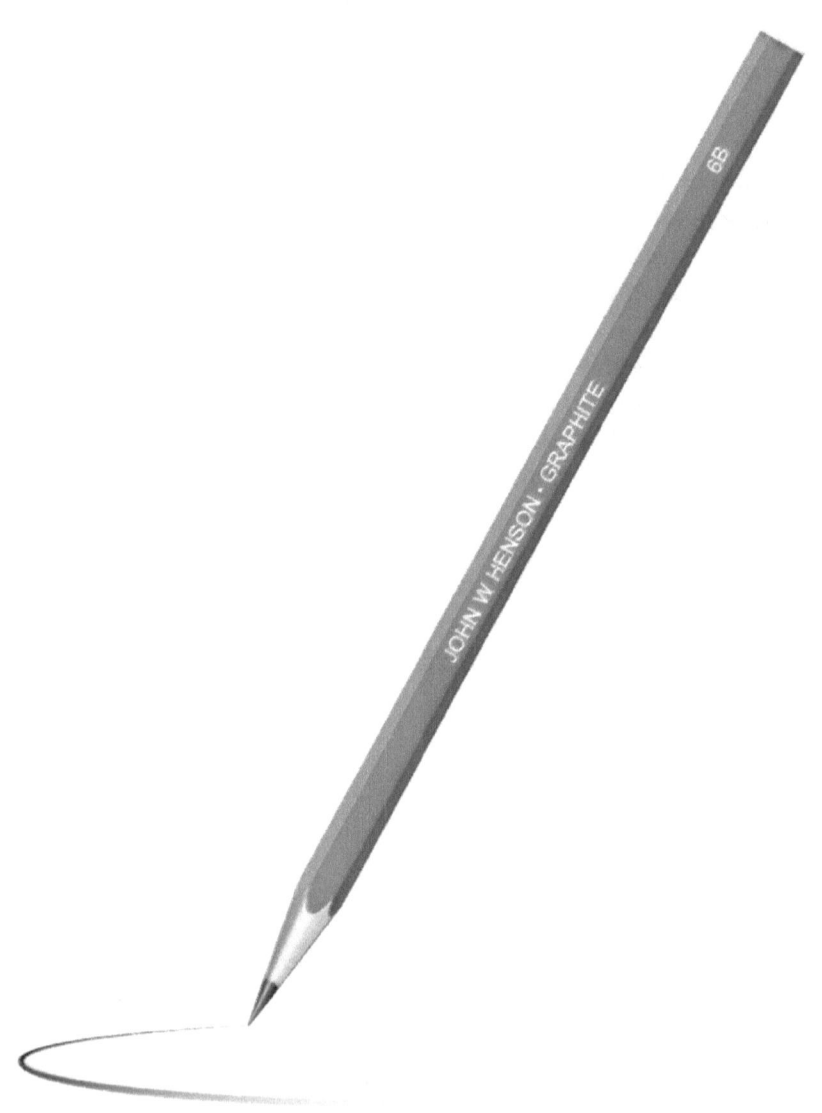

Portraits

Of family and friends

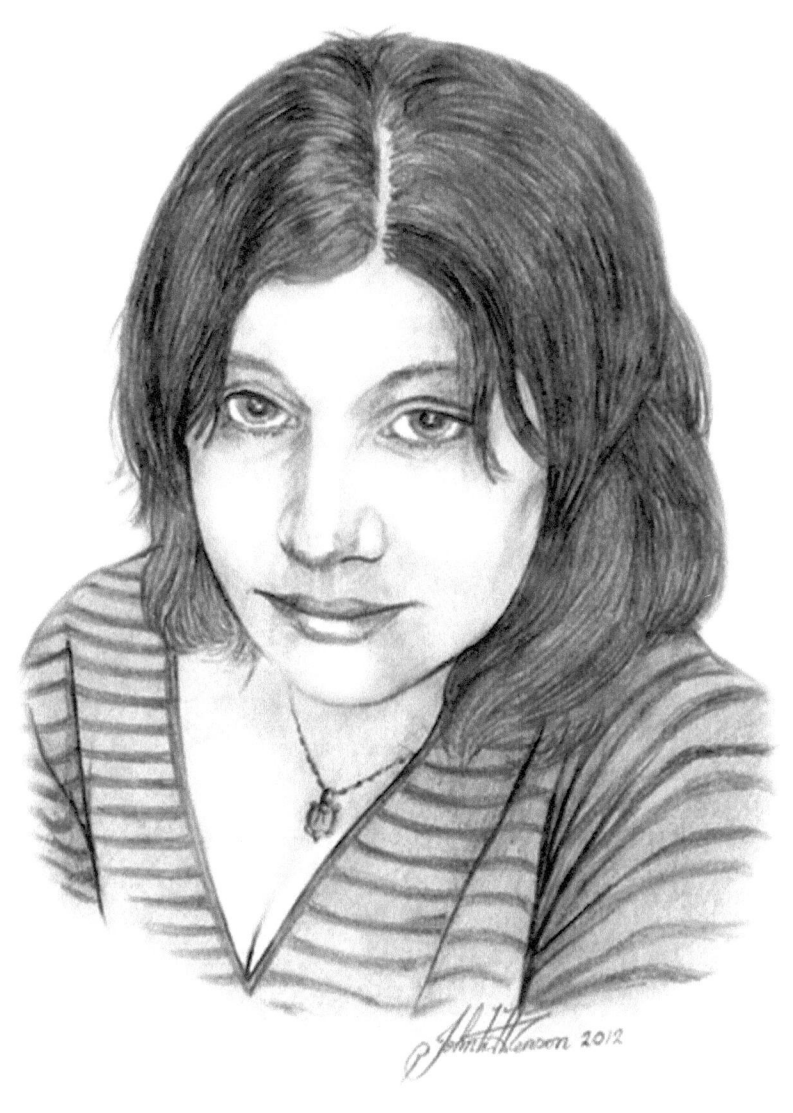

Ruth
A portrait of my beautiful daughter

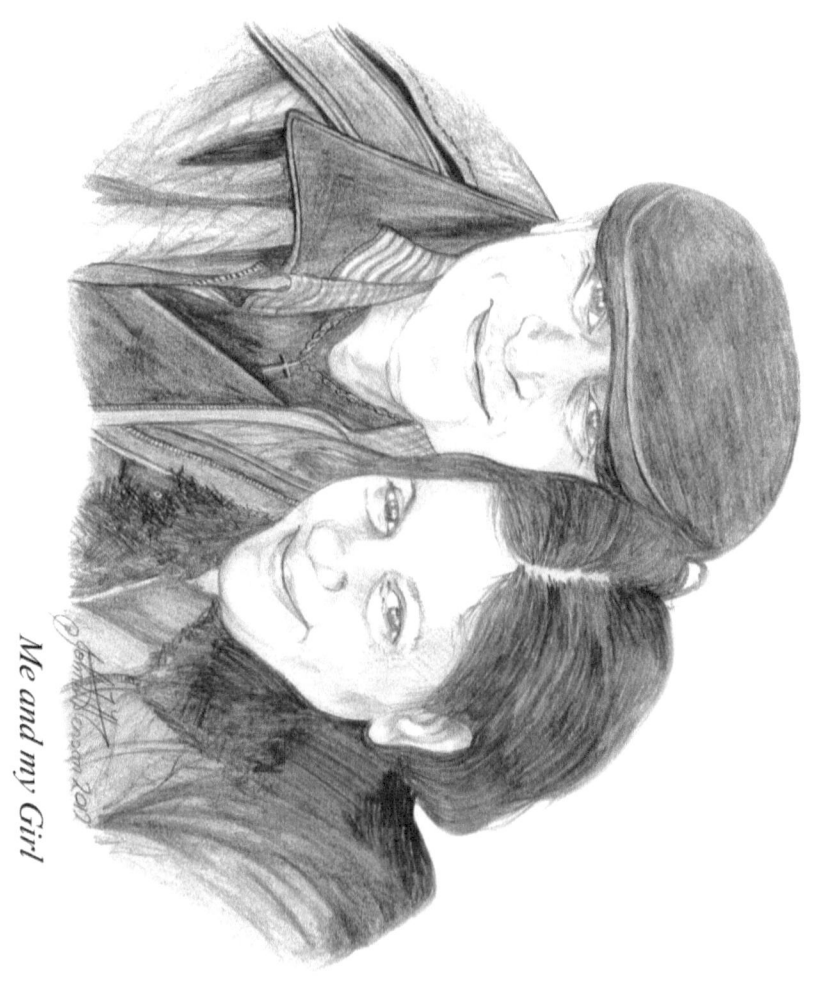

Me and my Girl

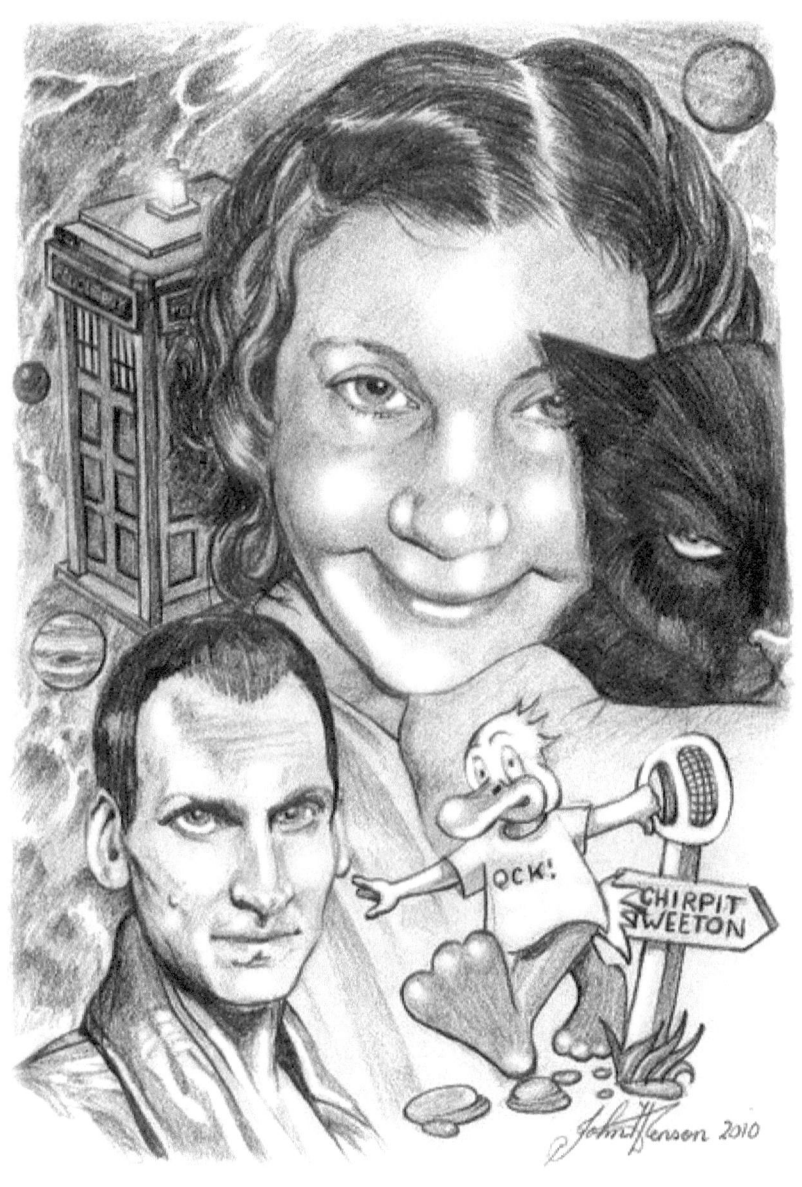

Ruth's World
A montage of things that make her happy

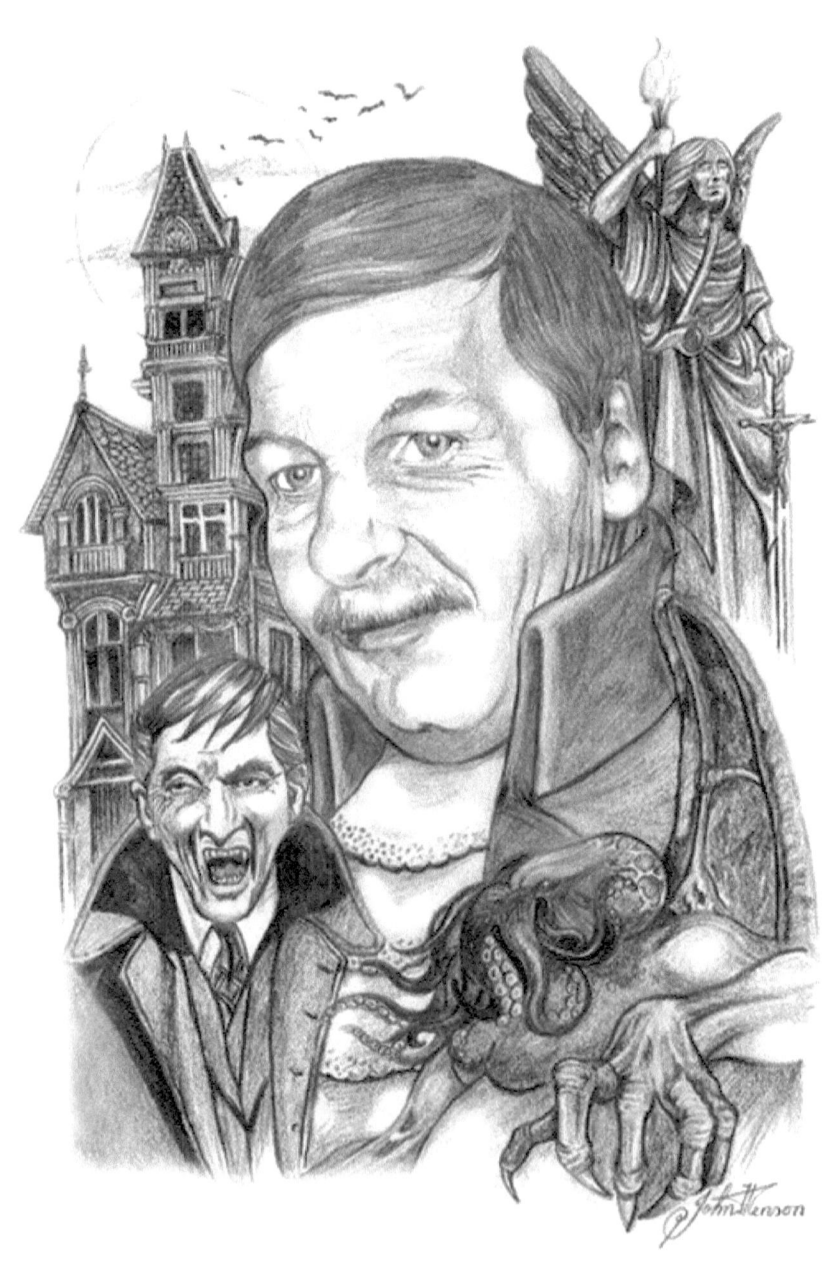

Mathew's World
A fan of the Macabre

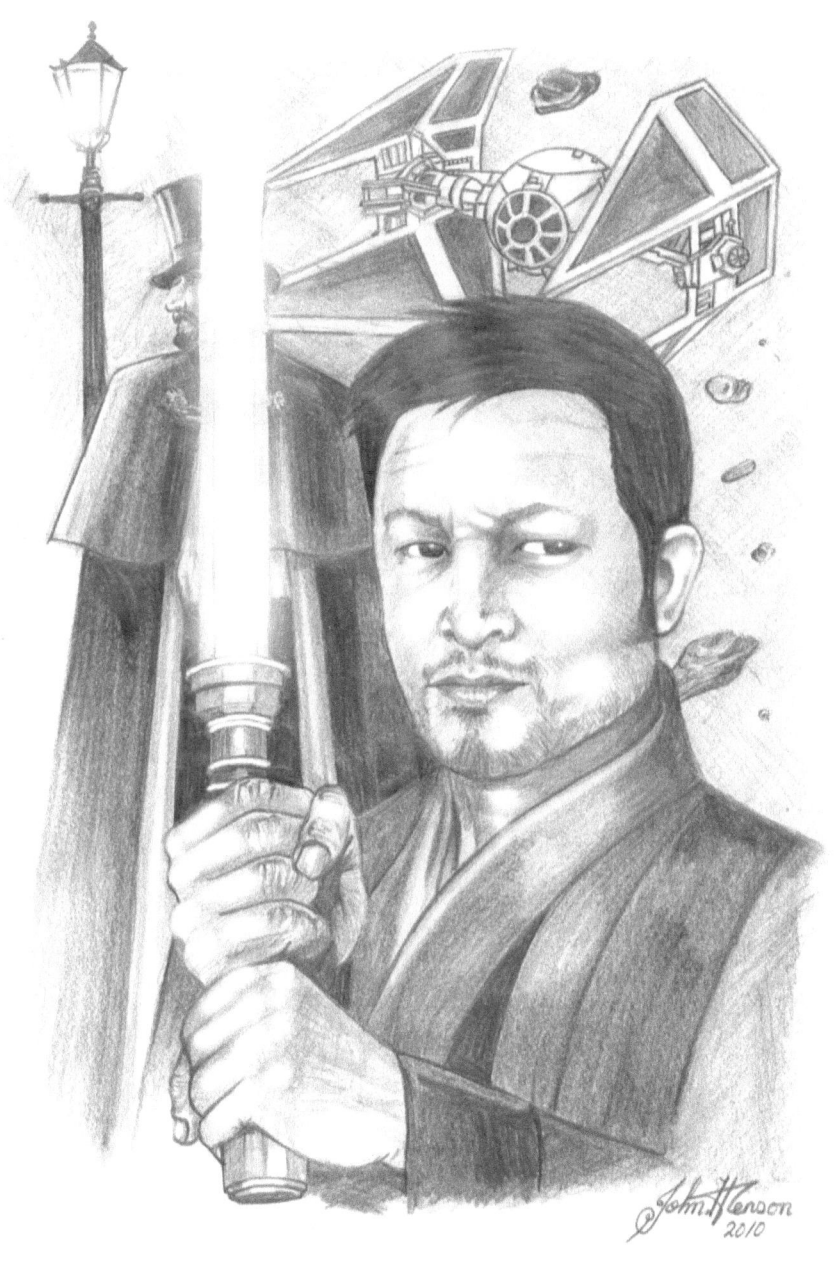

David

Star Wars and Jack the Ripper for my son

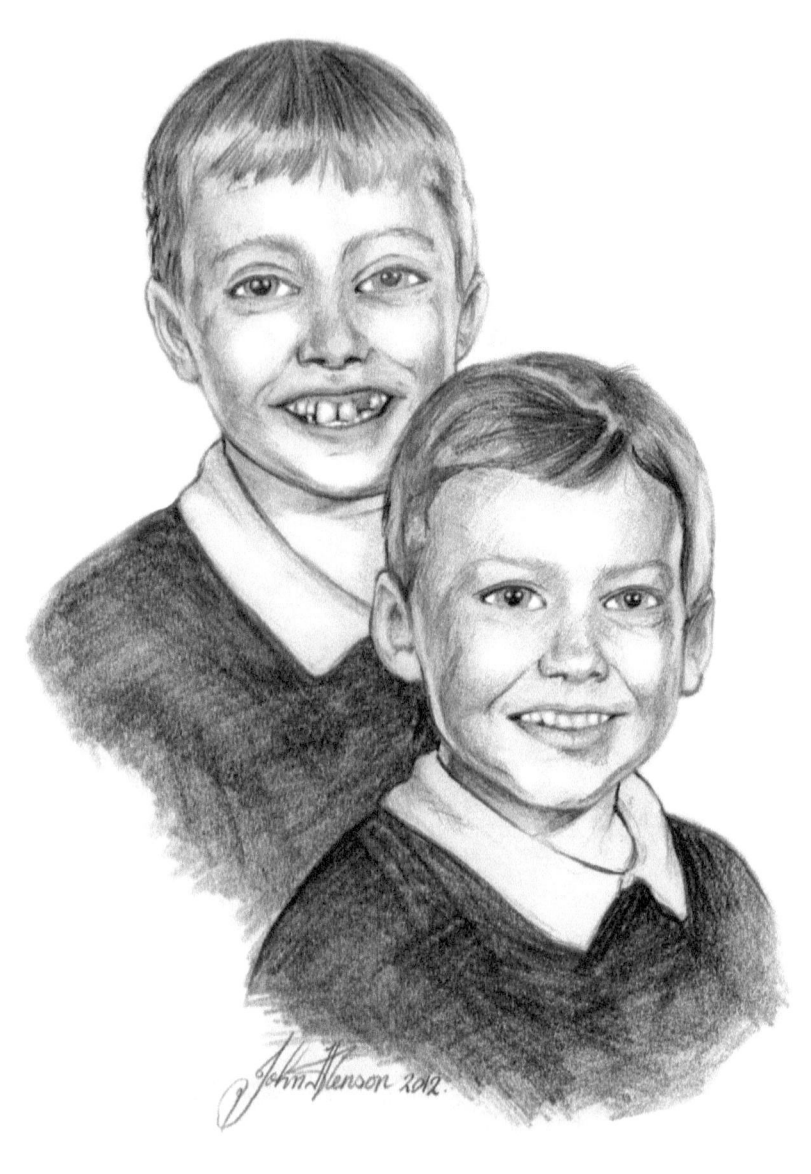

James and Joshua

Double trouble my daughter's nephews

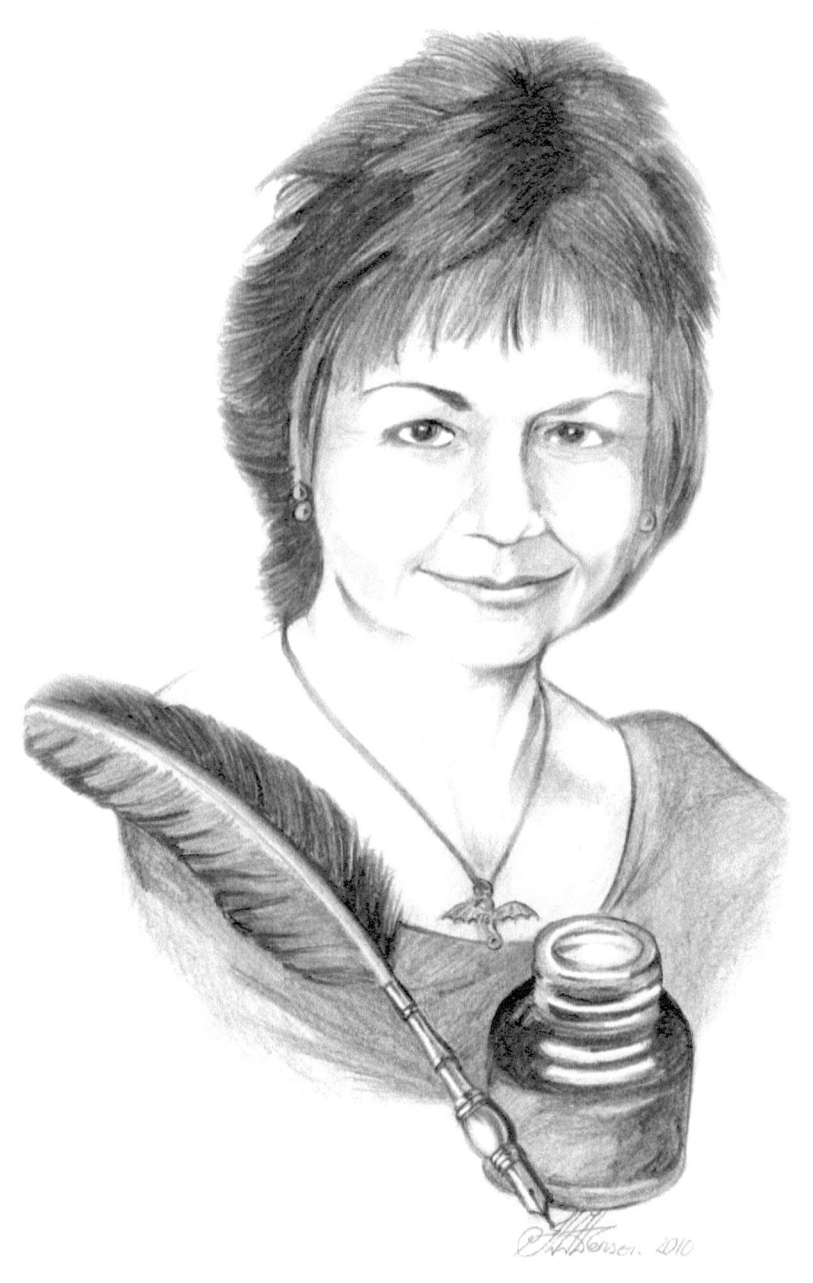

Paulette
My beloved fellow writer and artist Paulette Kosak

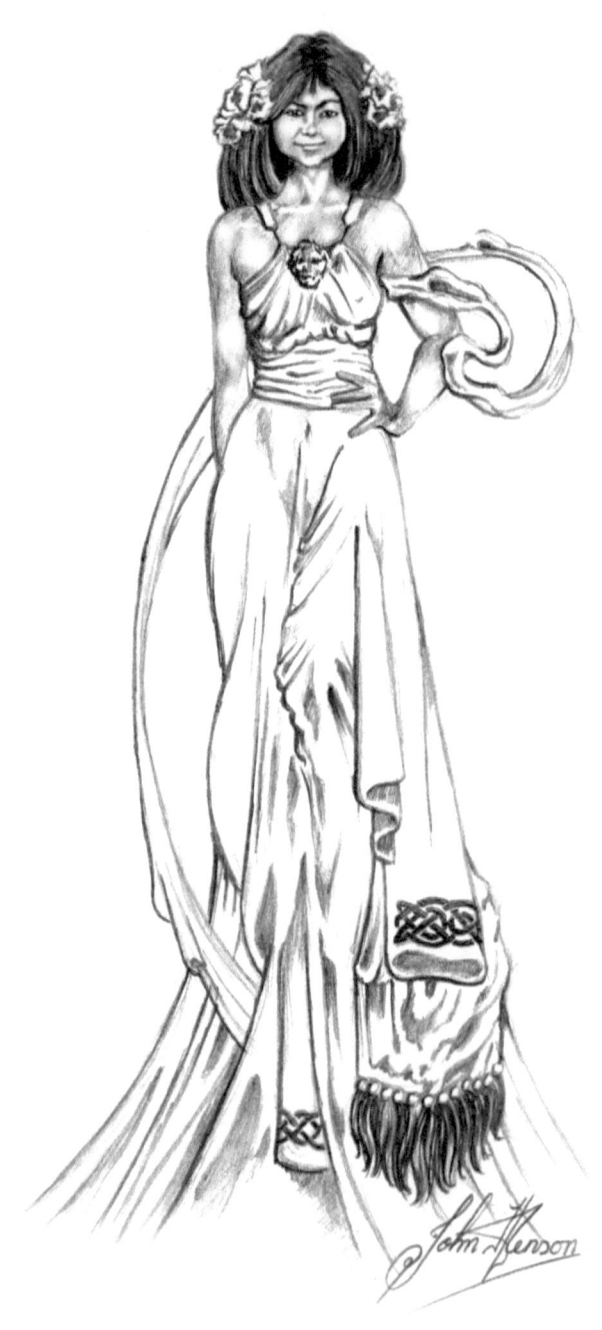

The Inner Celt
Paulette Kosak

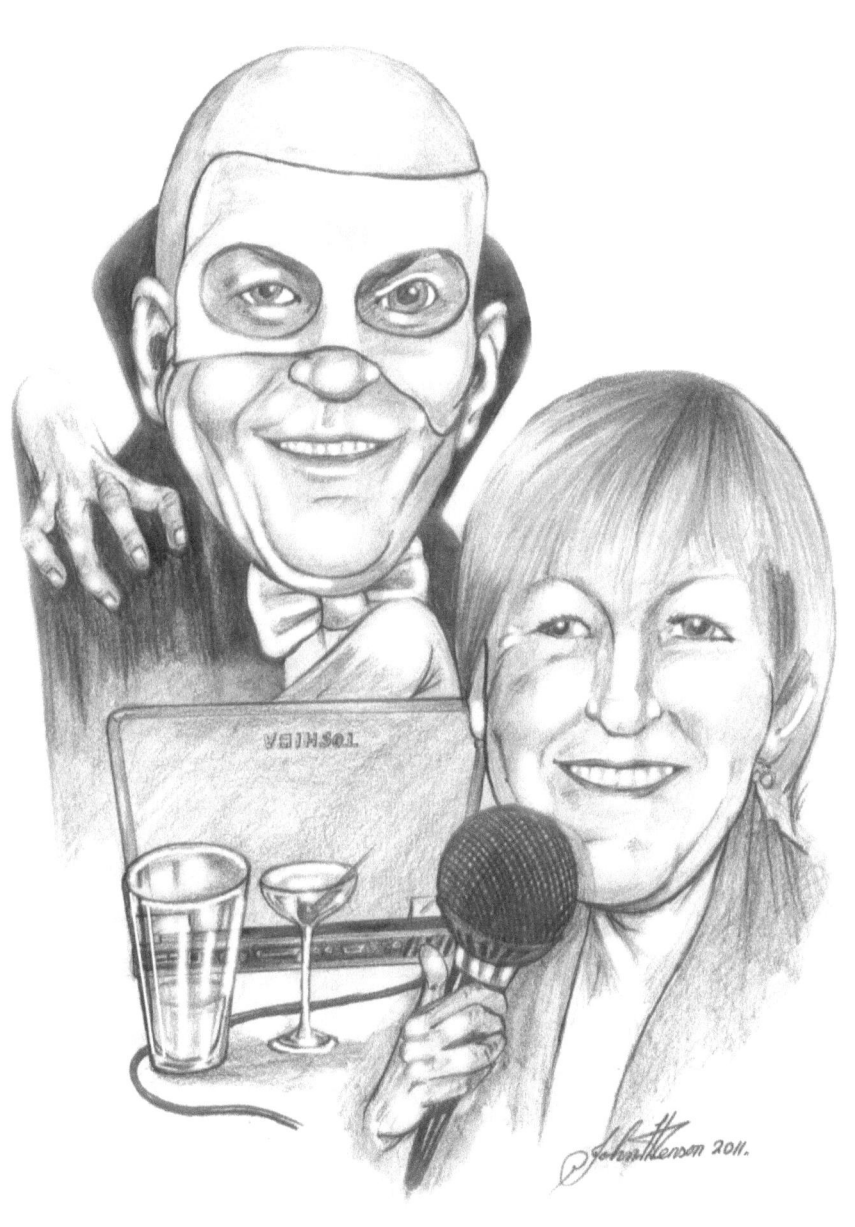

Phantom of the Karaoke
Friends Bob and Linda

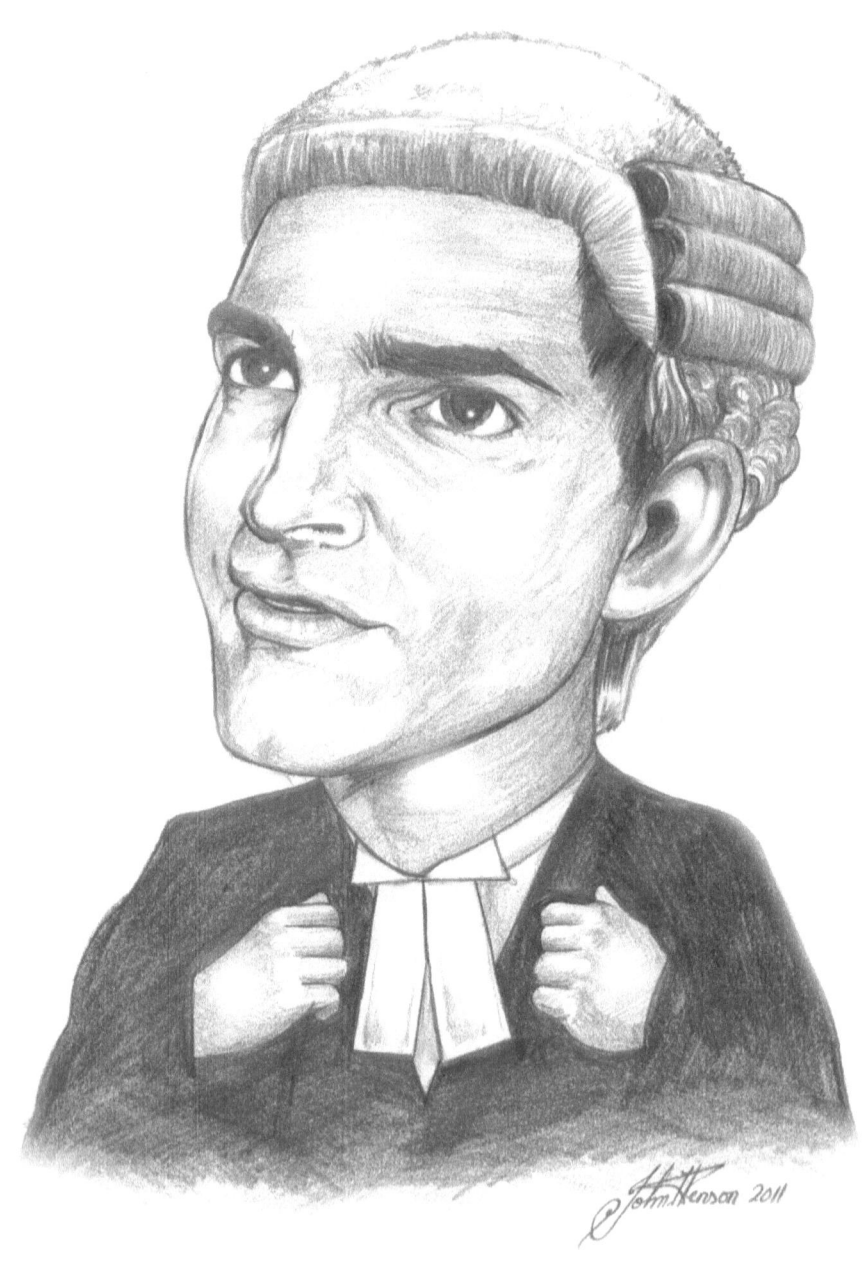

David Bennet QC

Hanging in his chambers at the Old Bailey

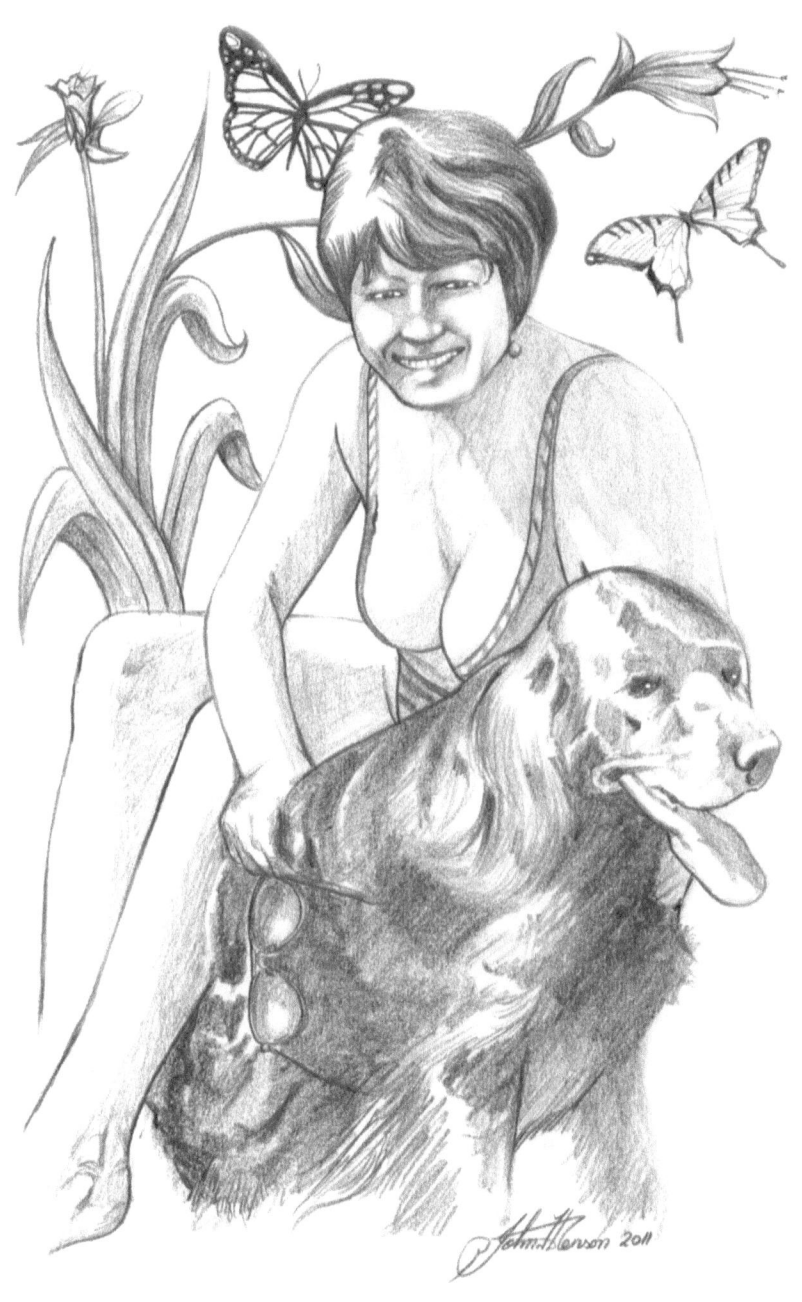

Beryl with Setter
For my friend Charles, his deceased wife

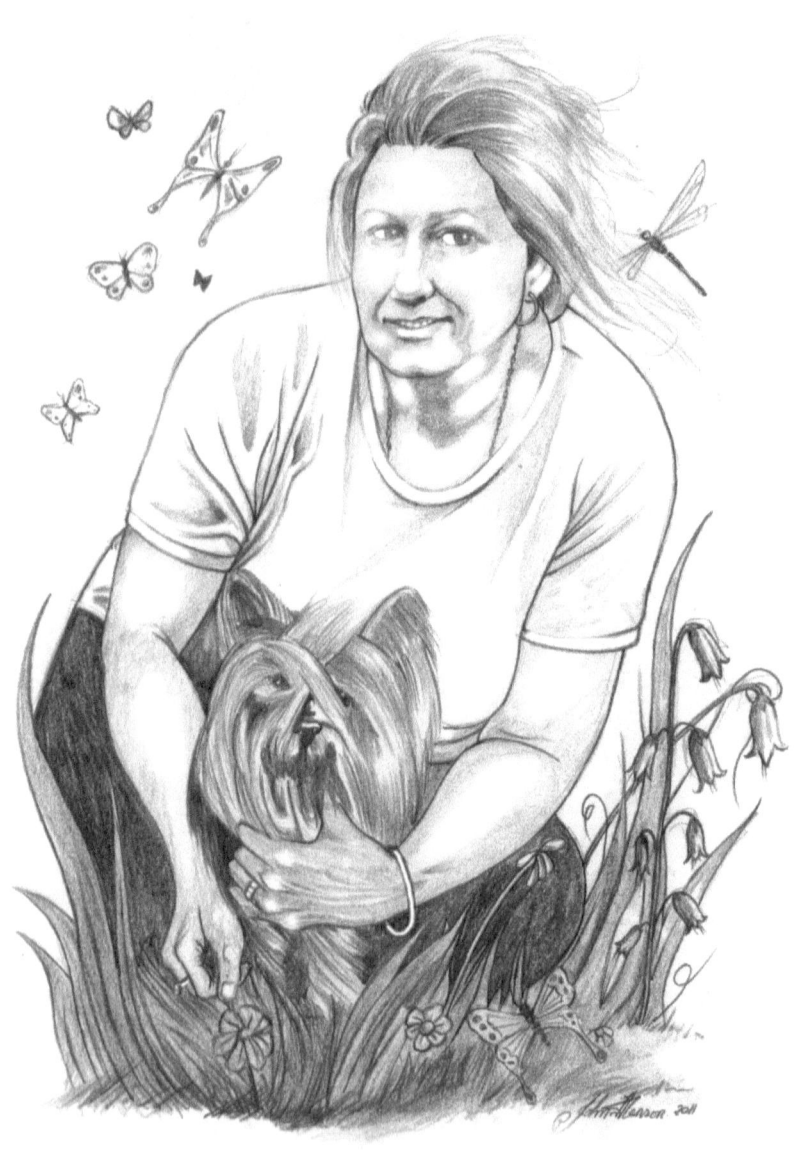

Beryl with Yorkie

She loved her dogs

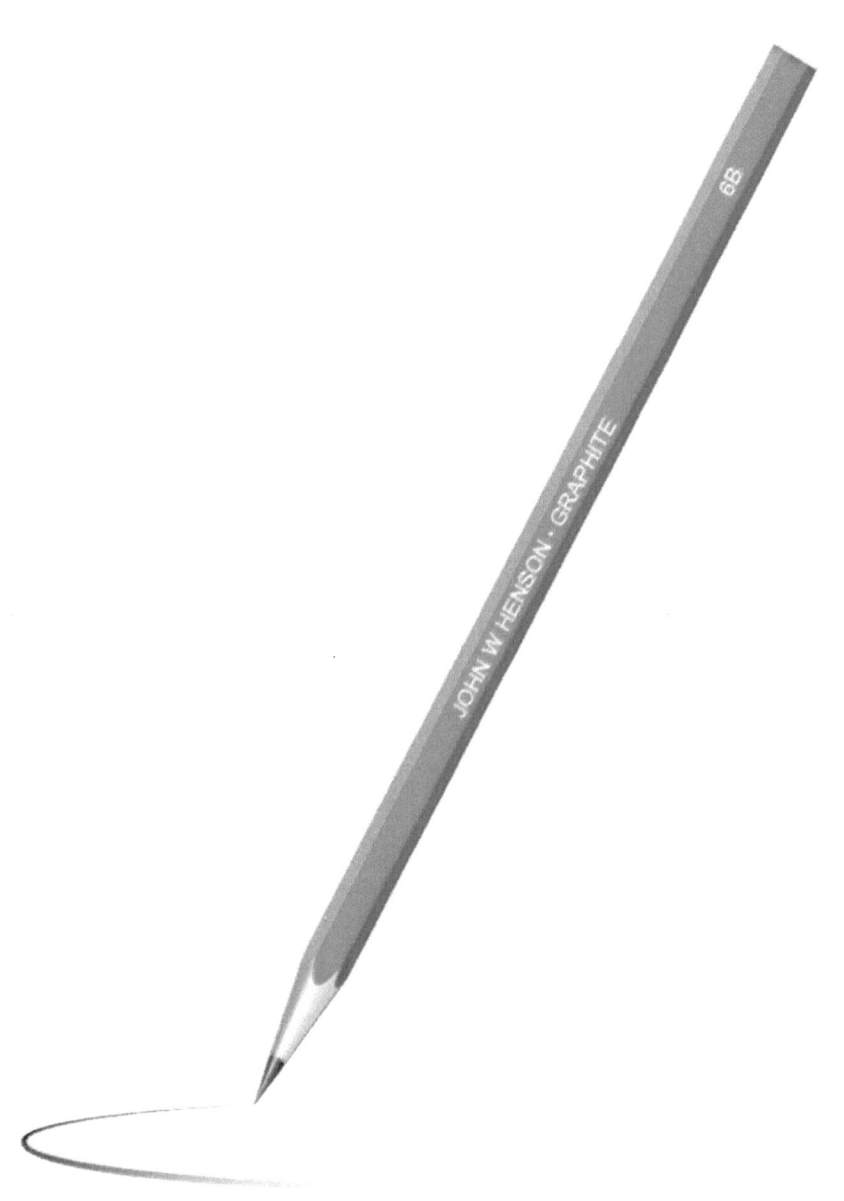

Animals

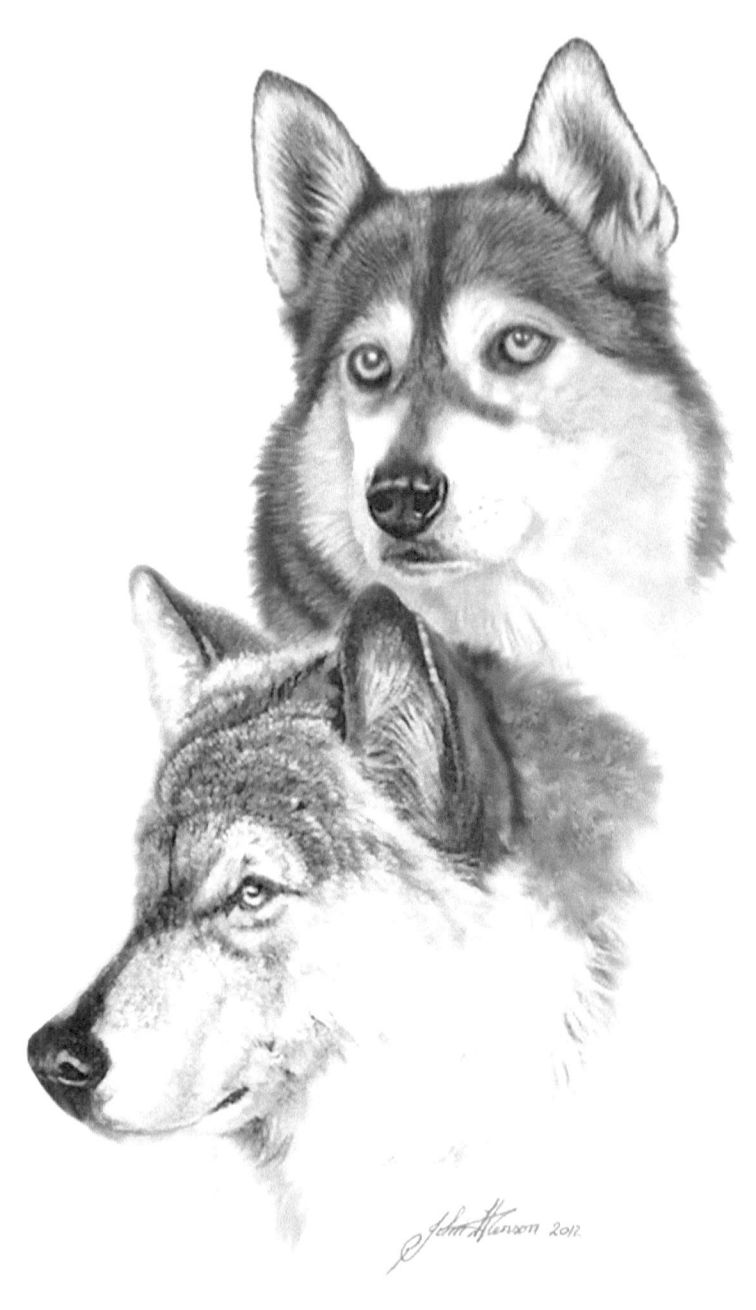

Chi Chi and Nanook

My beloved Huskies

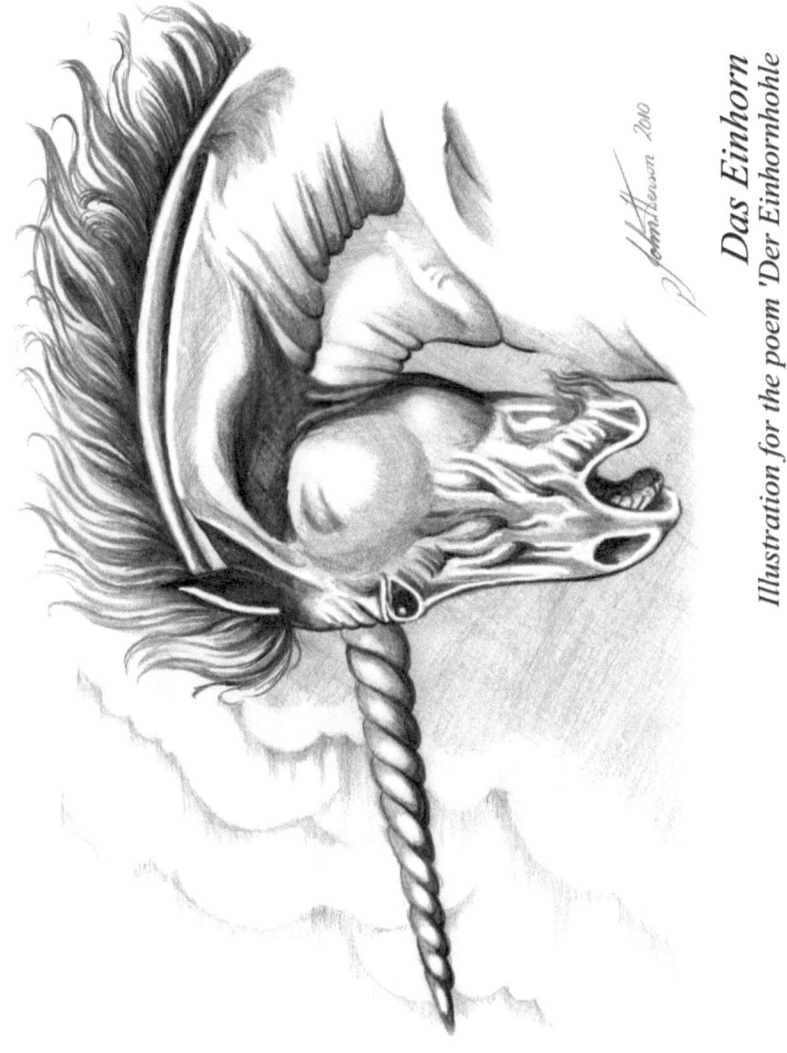

Das Einhorn

Illustration for the poem 'Der Einhornhohle

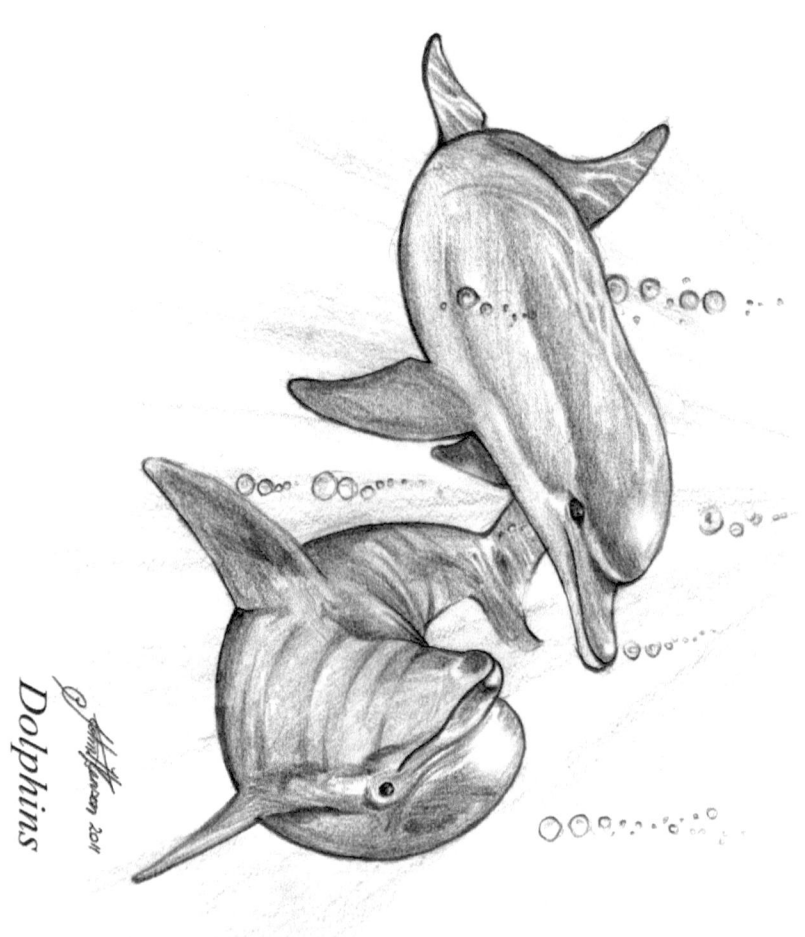

Dolphins

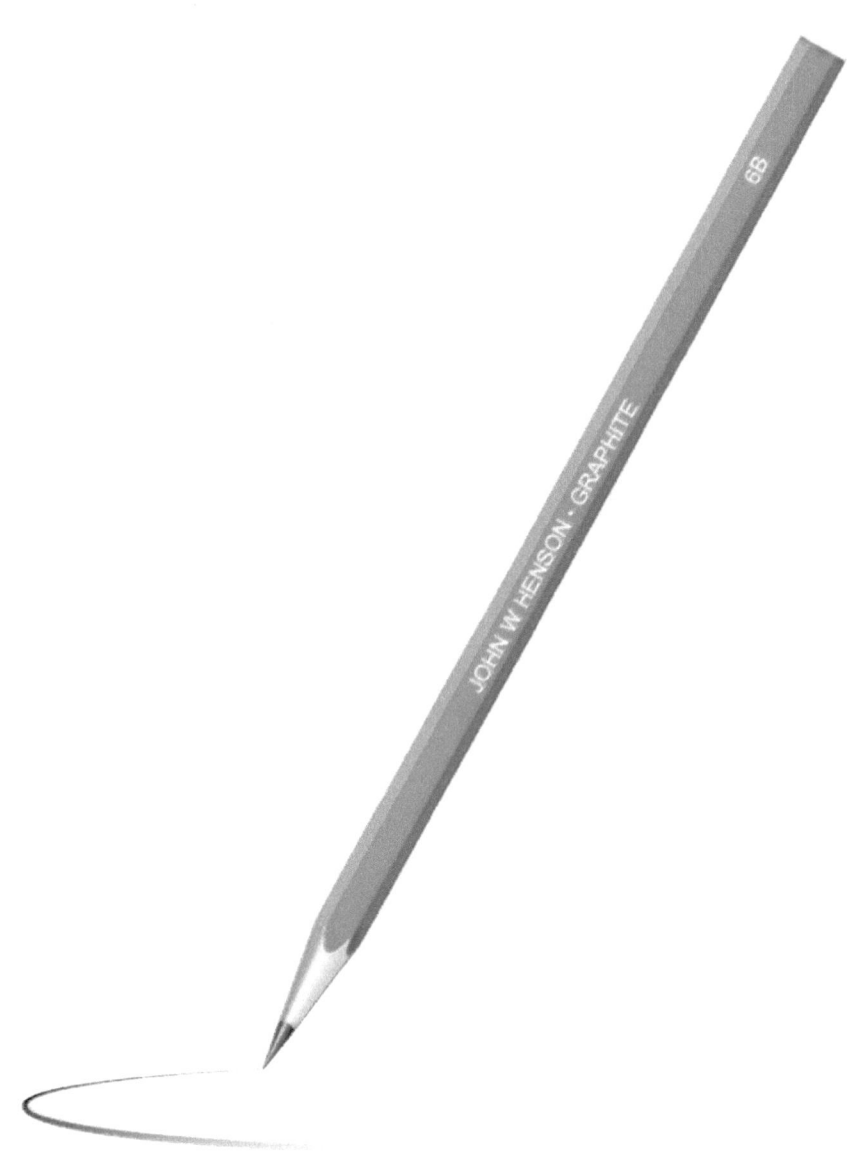

Celebrities

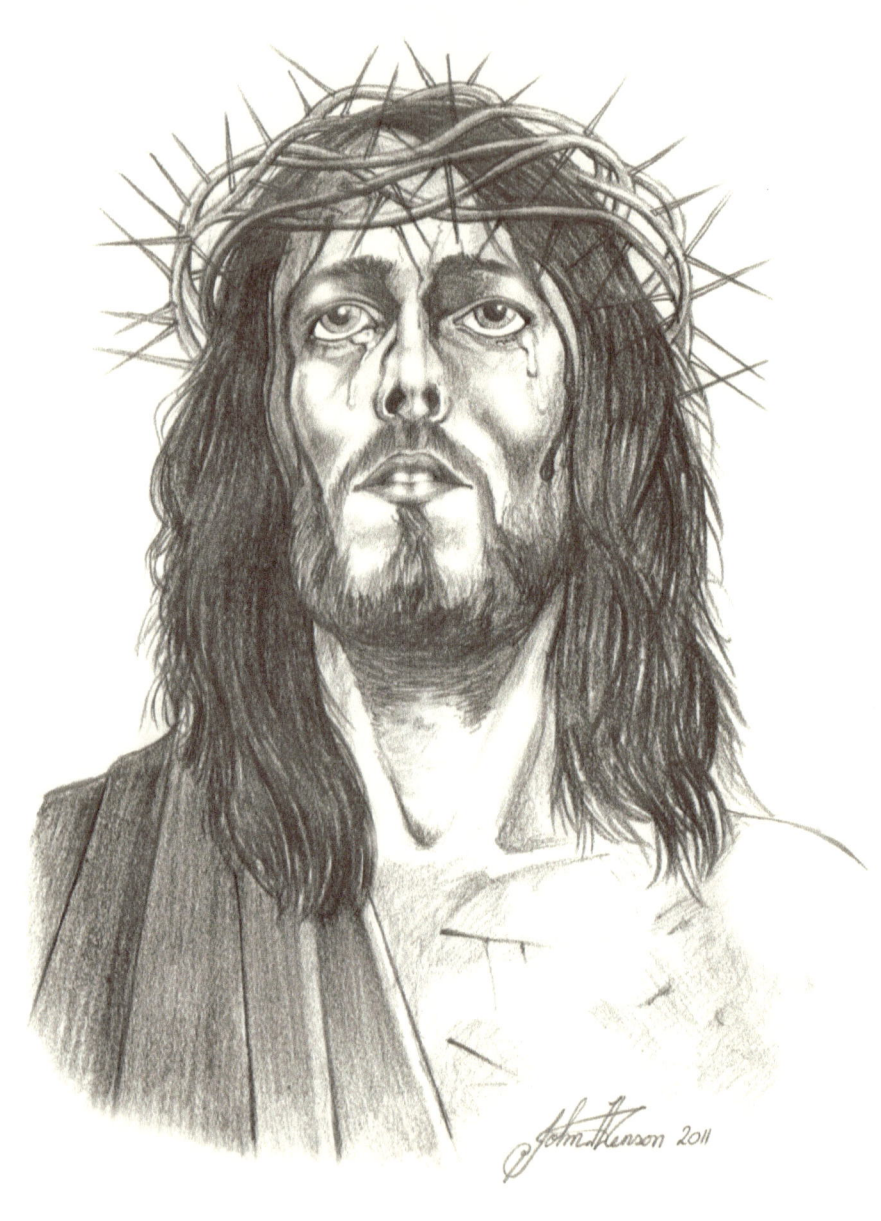

Jesus of Nazareth

Robert Powell

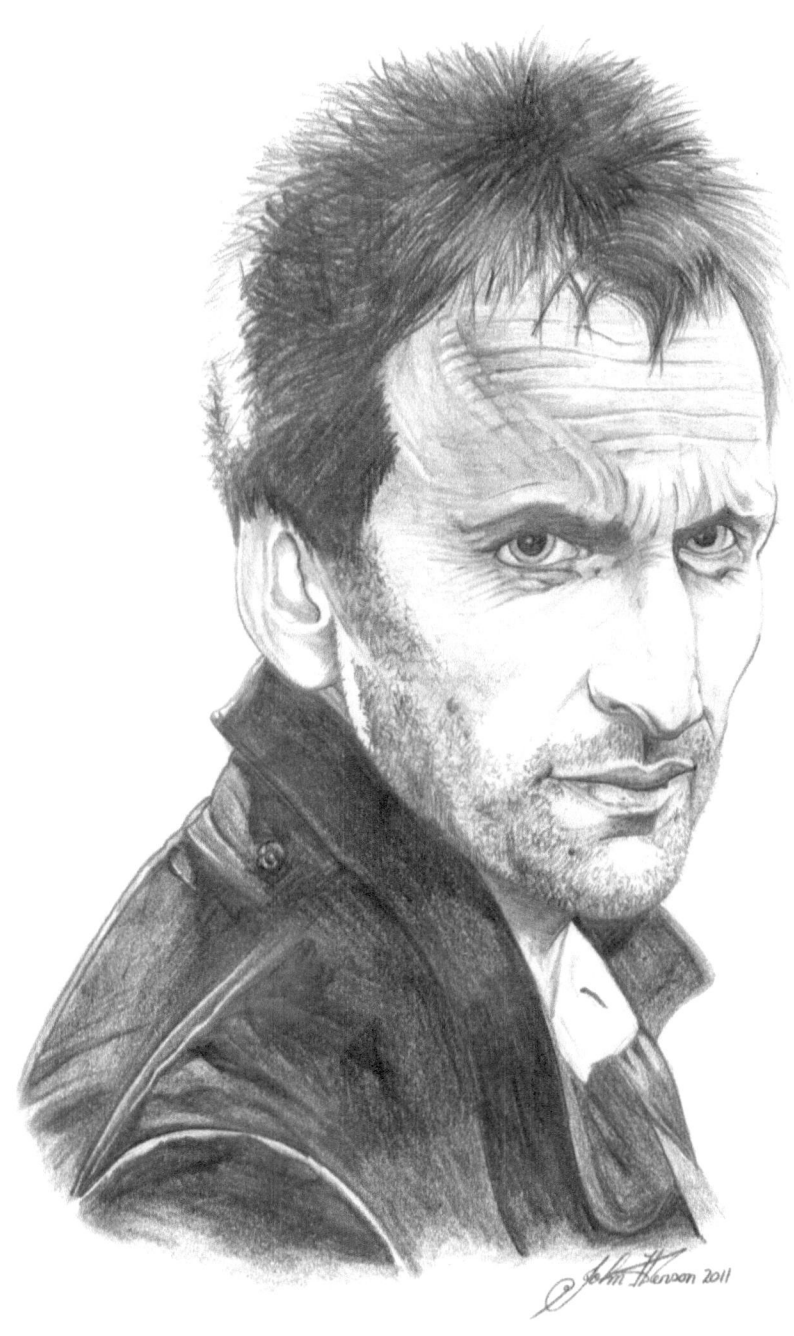

Leo

Christopher Eccleston as Leo

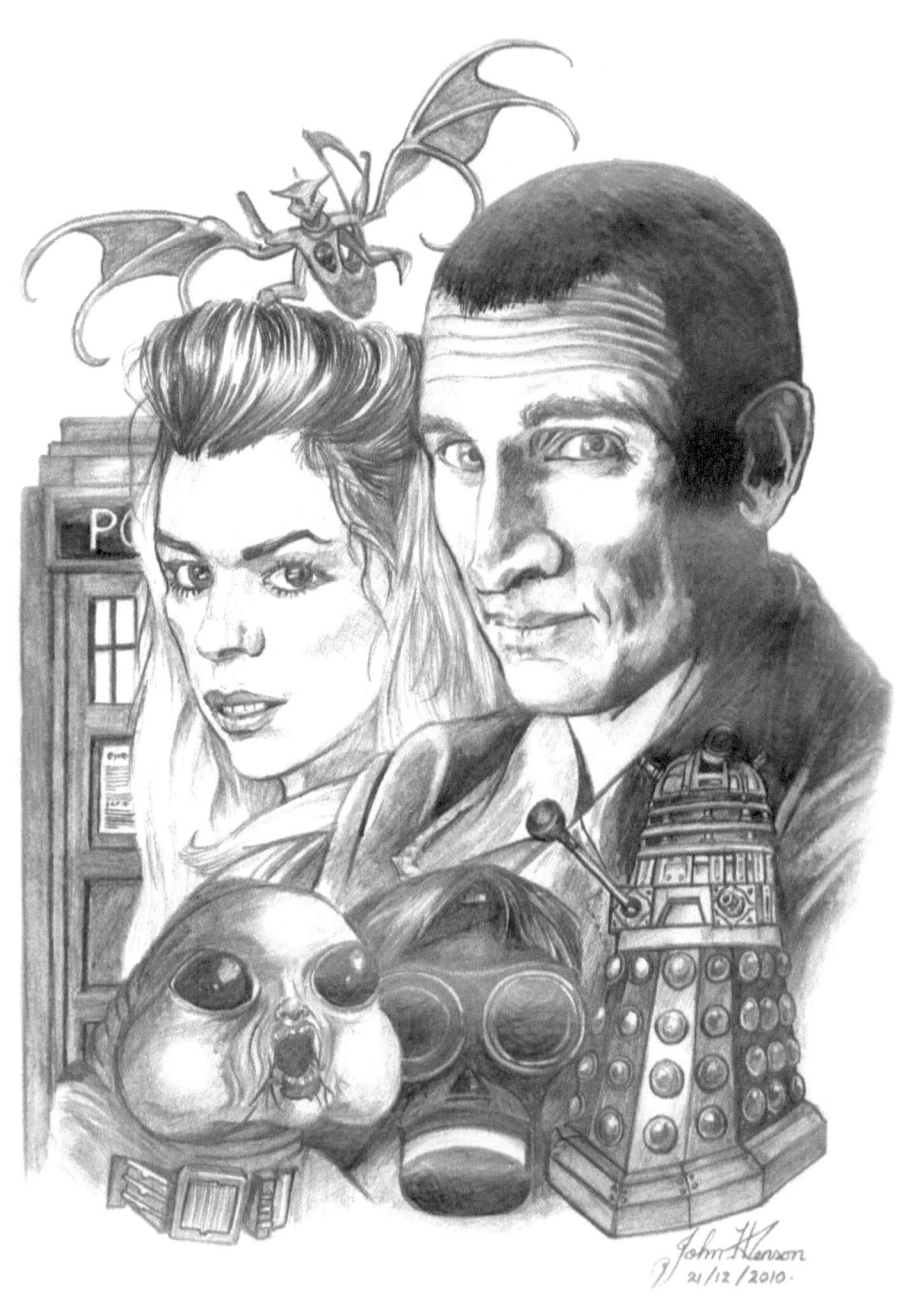

Dr Who
Christopher Eccleston and Billy Piper

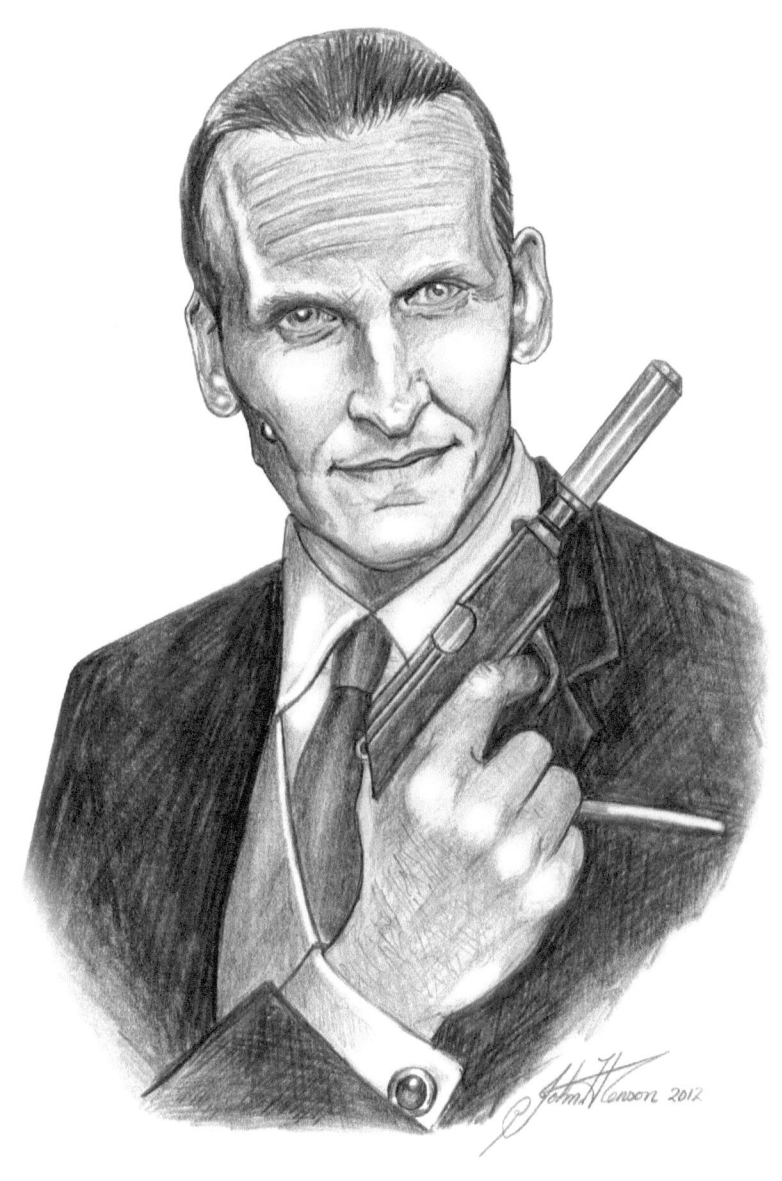

Eccleston Bond

Chris has always wanted to play Bond

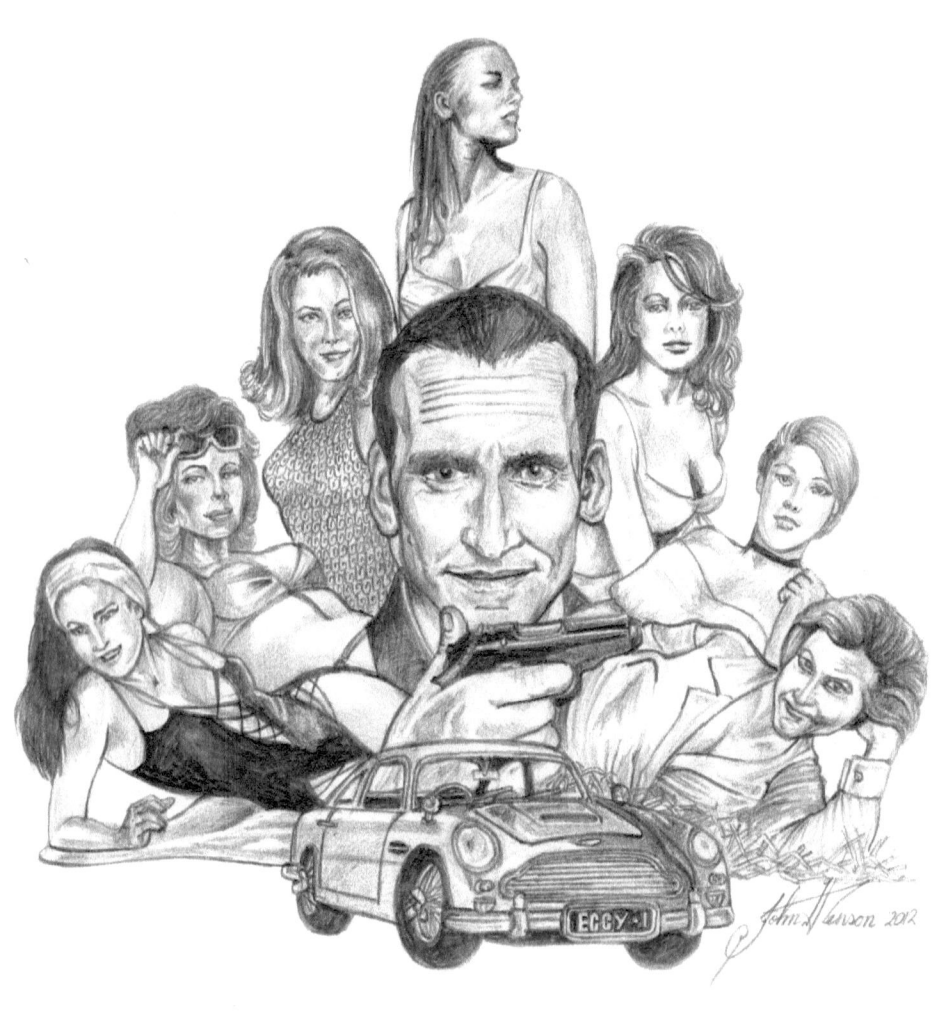

A Northern Bond
One with the girls

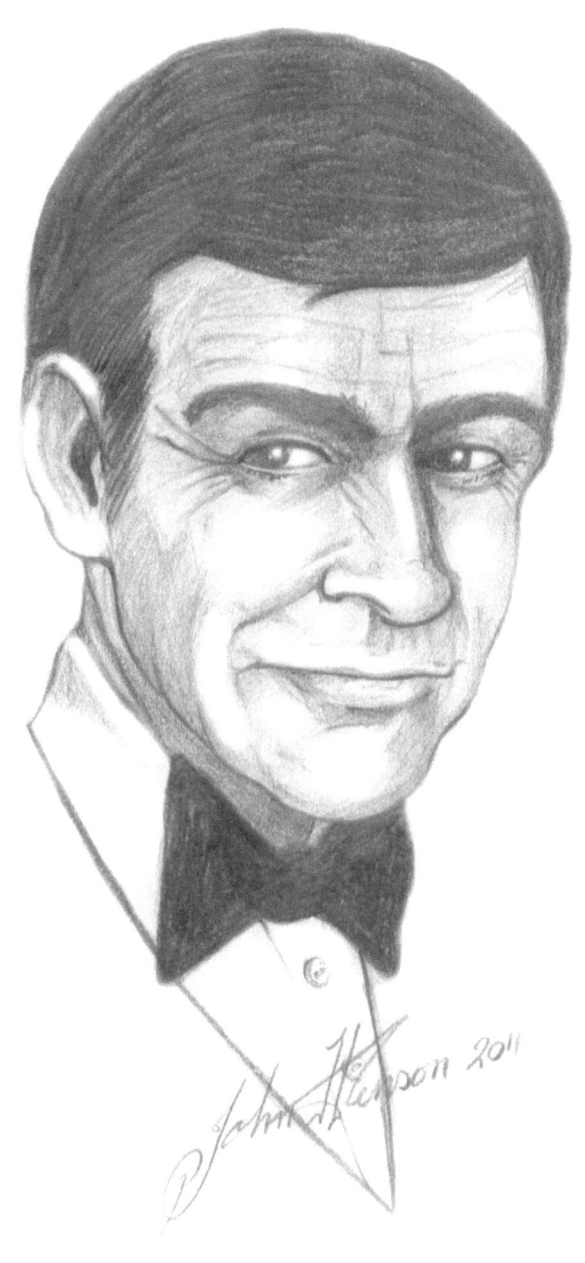

Bond
Sean Connery

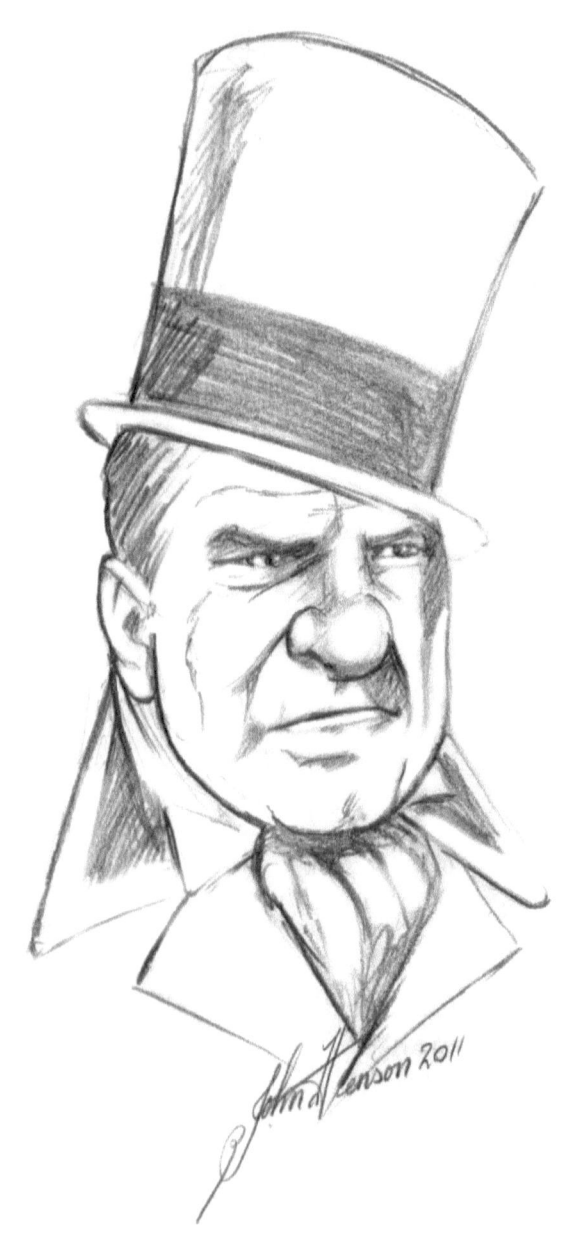

Mr. Micawber
W.C. Fields

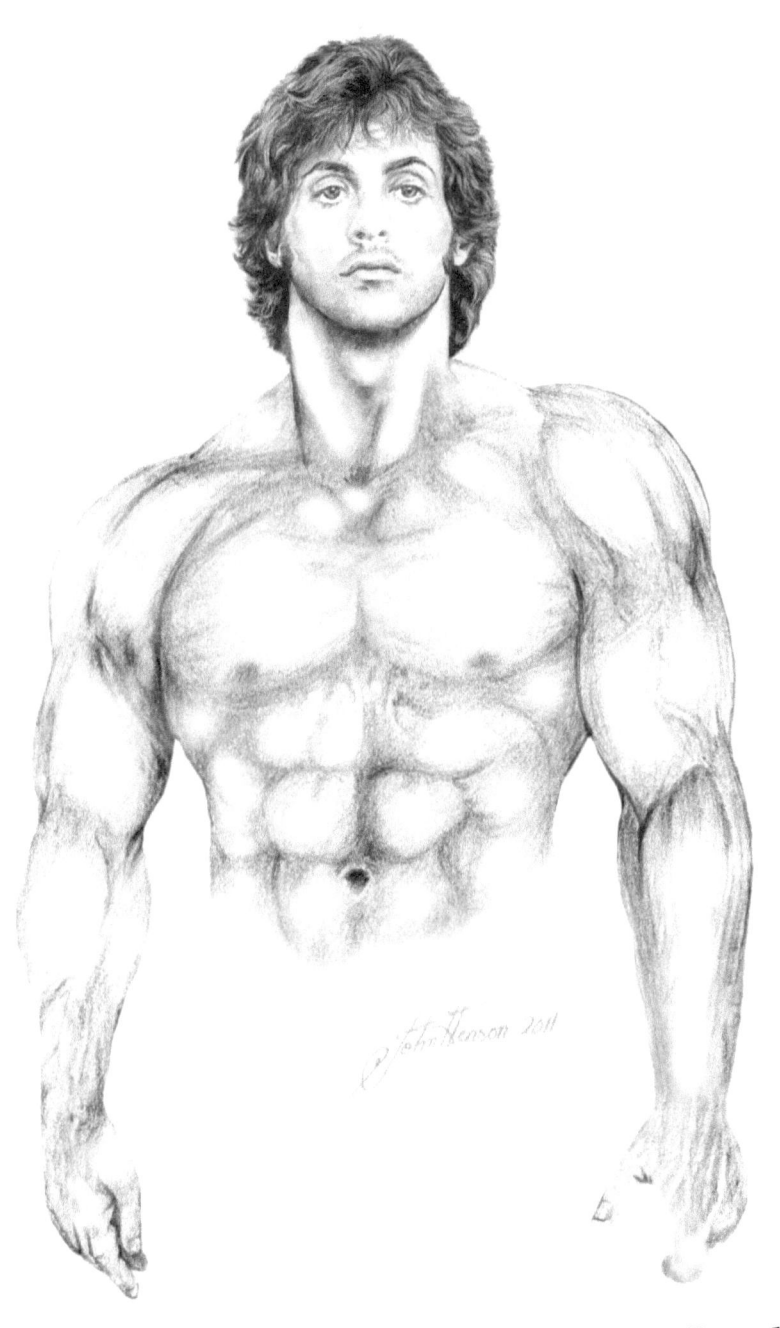

Rambo

Sylvester Stallone

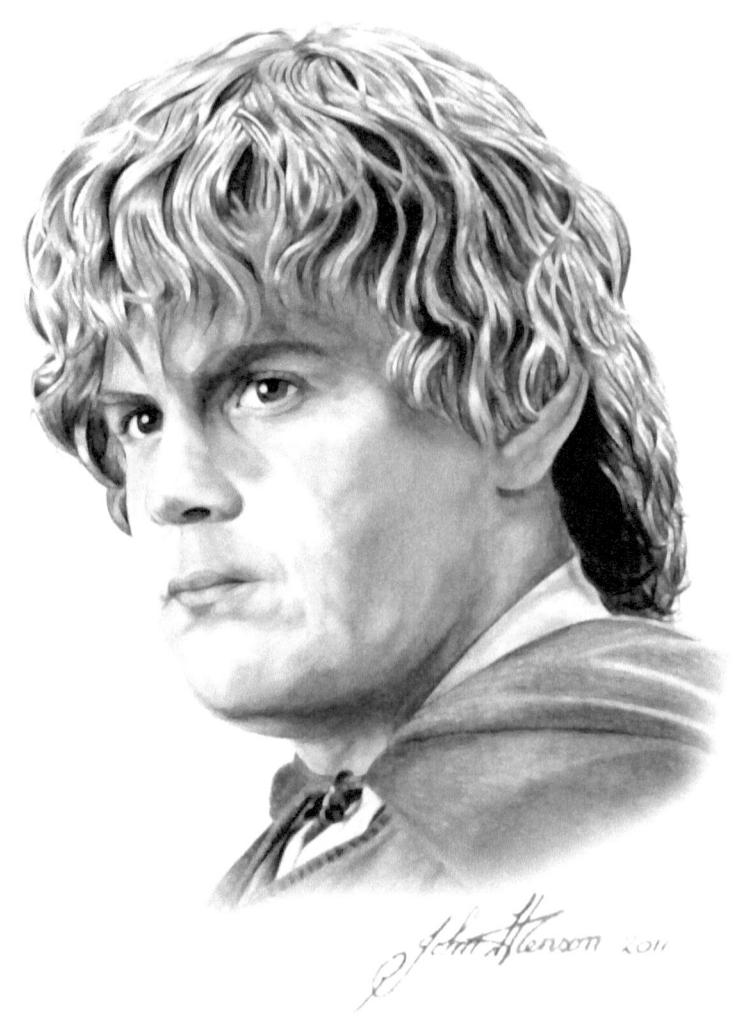

Sam
Sean Astin

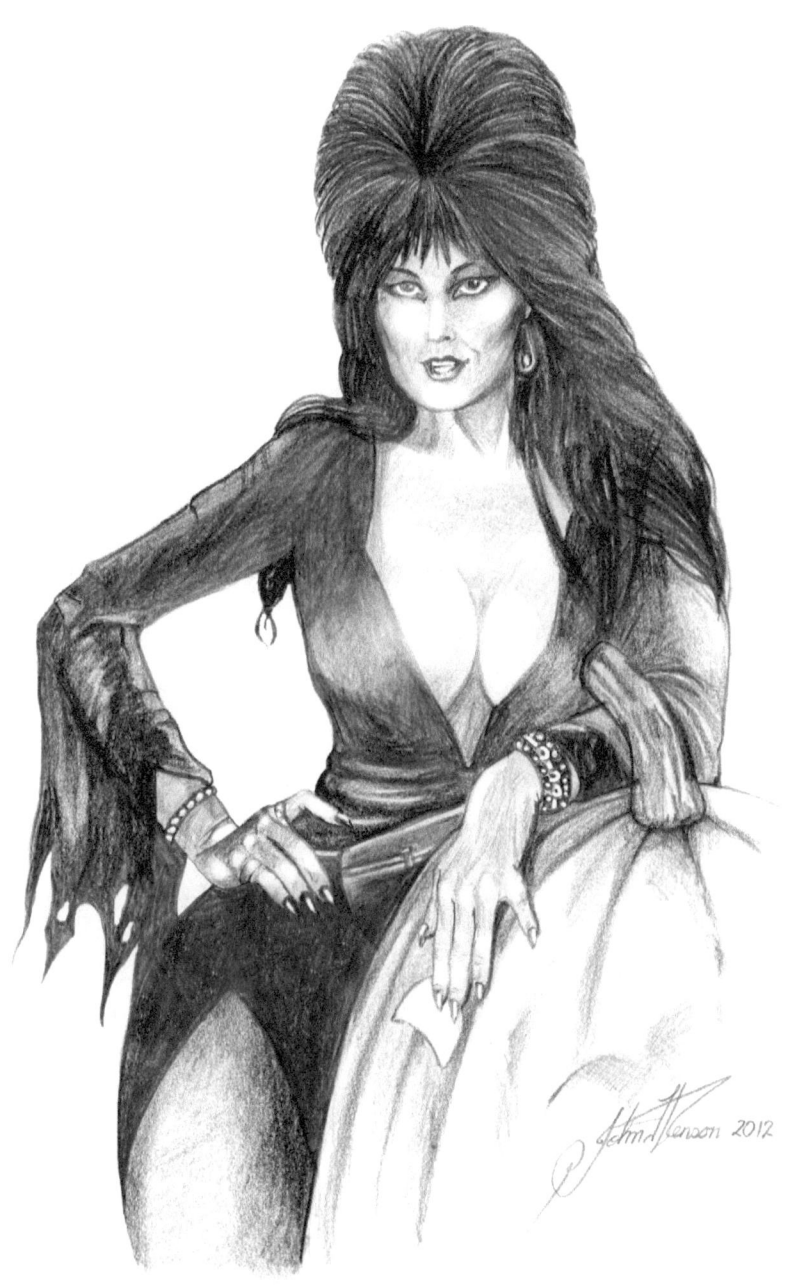

Elvira
Mistress of the Dark

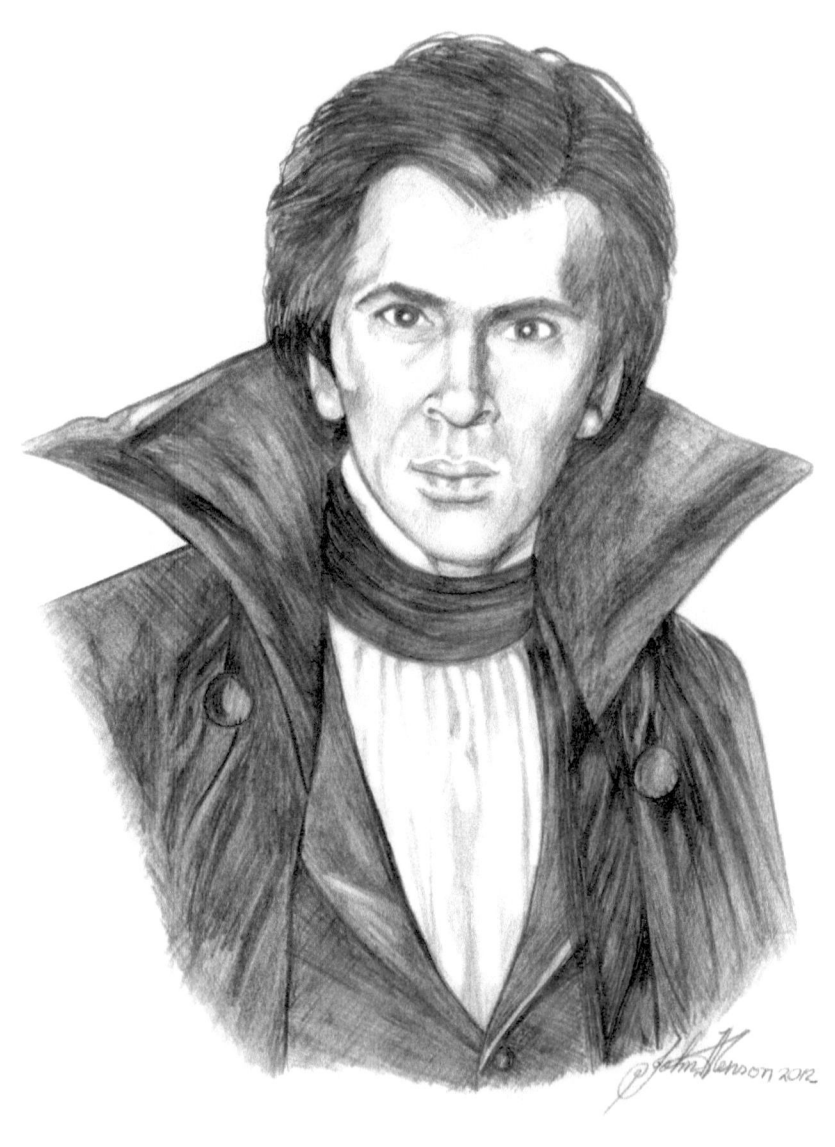

Count Dracula
Frank Langella

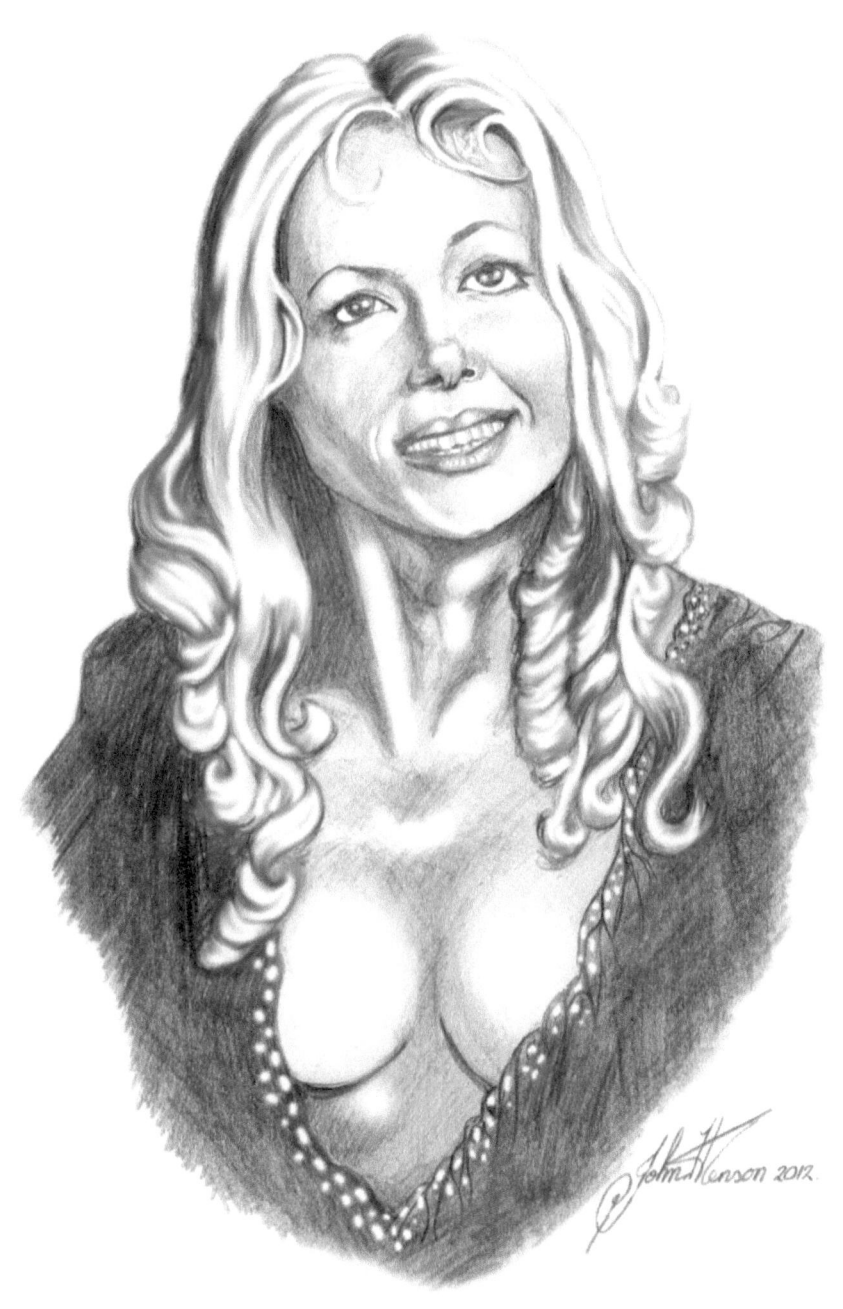

Countess Dracula
Ingrid Pitt

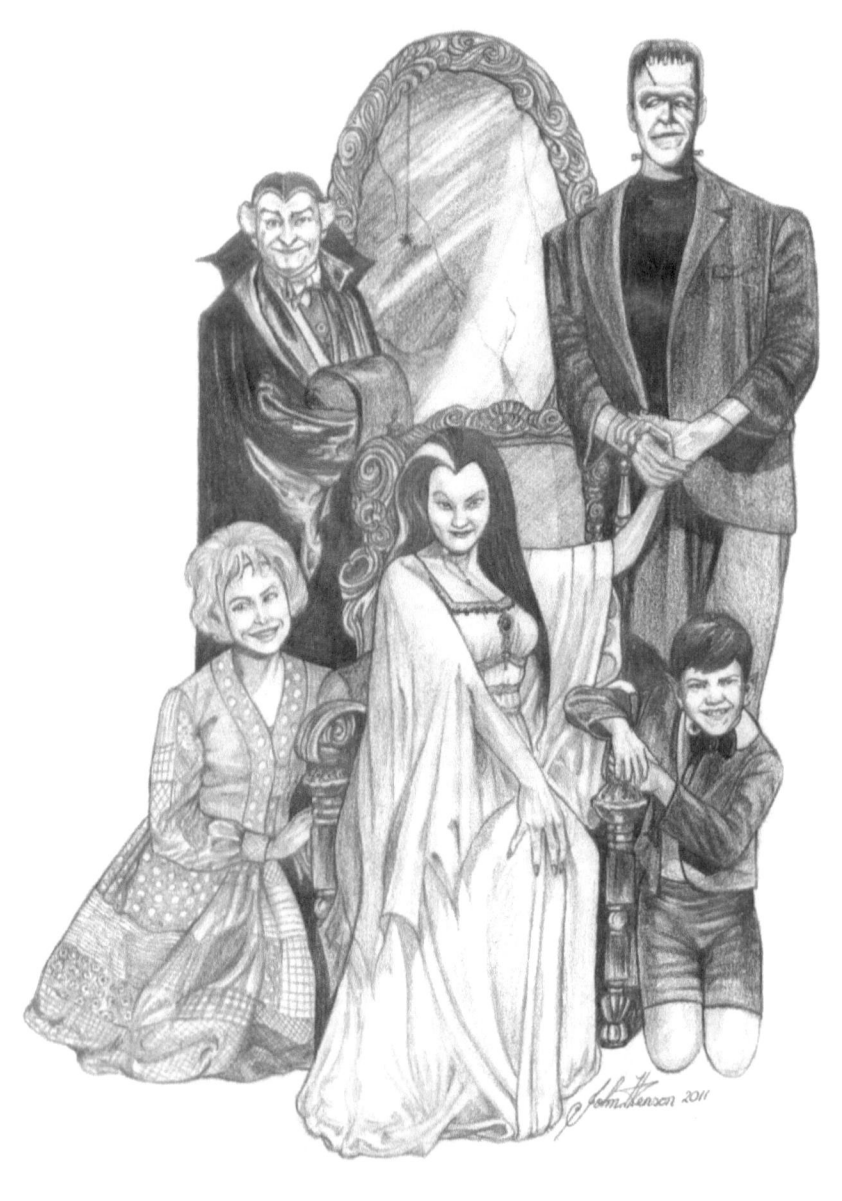

The Munsters
A lovely family

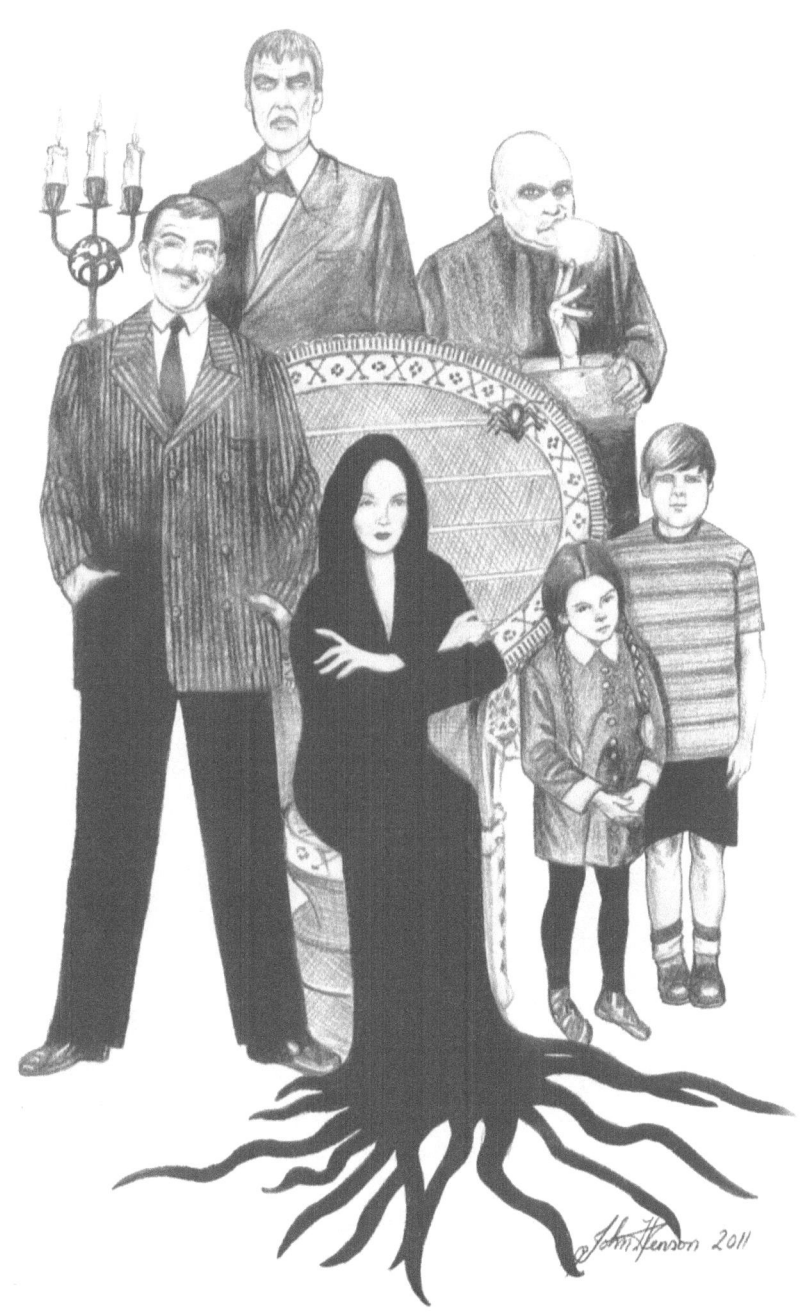

The Addams Family
They're creepy and they're kooky

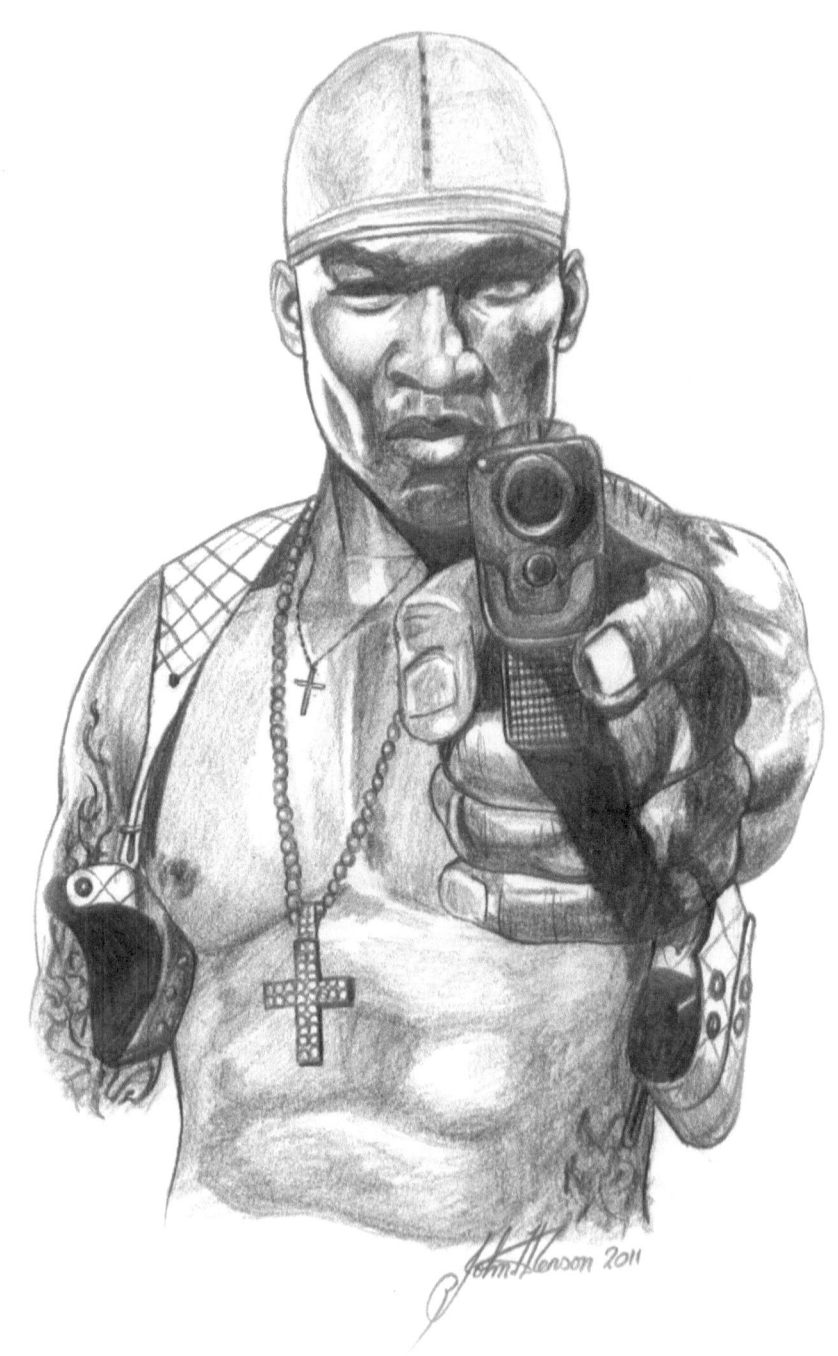

50 Cent

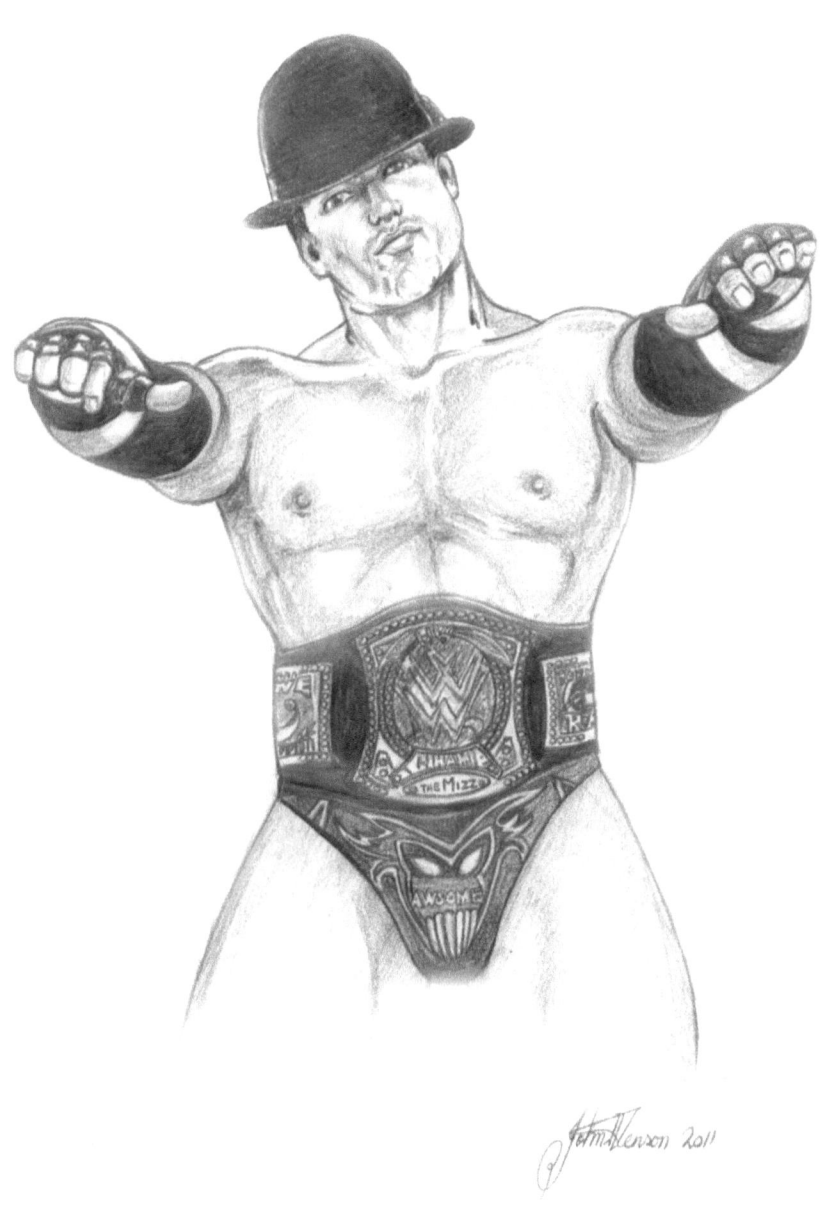

The Mizz

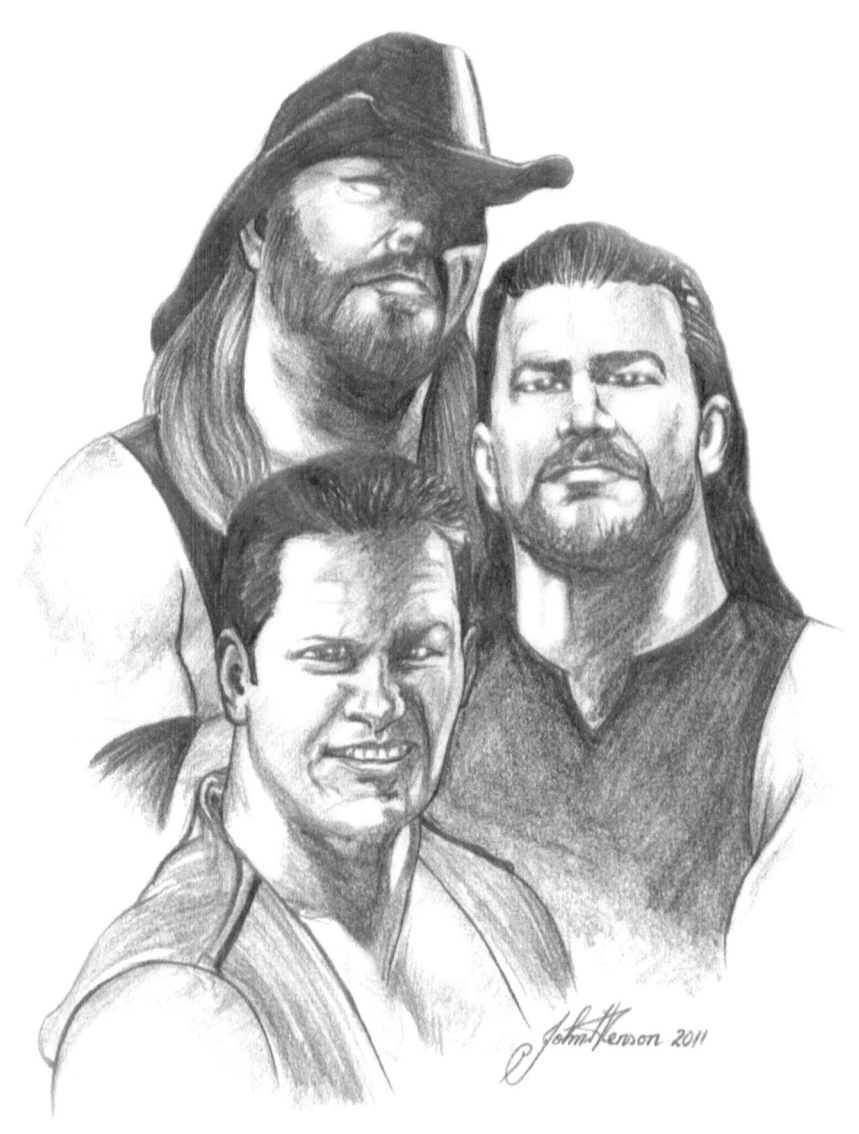

Wrestlers

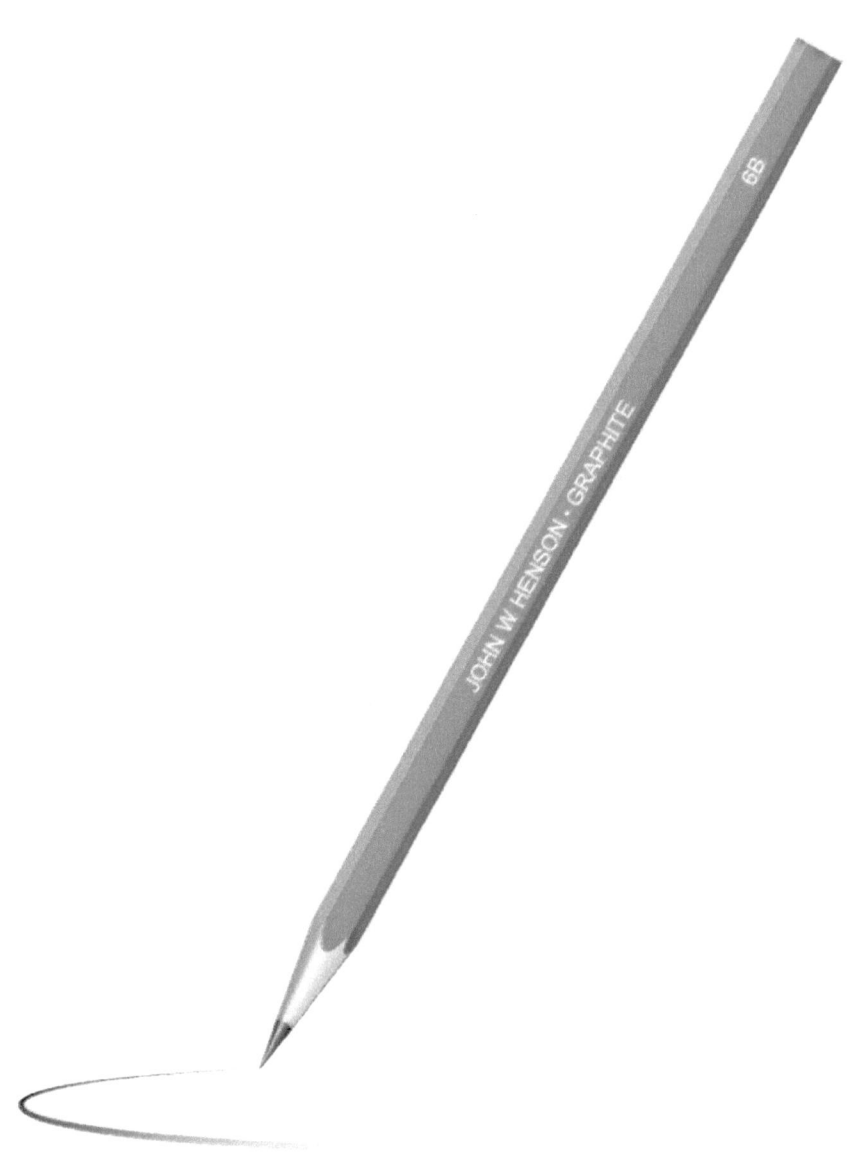

Horror

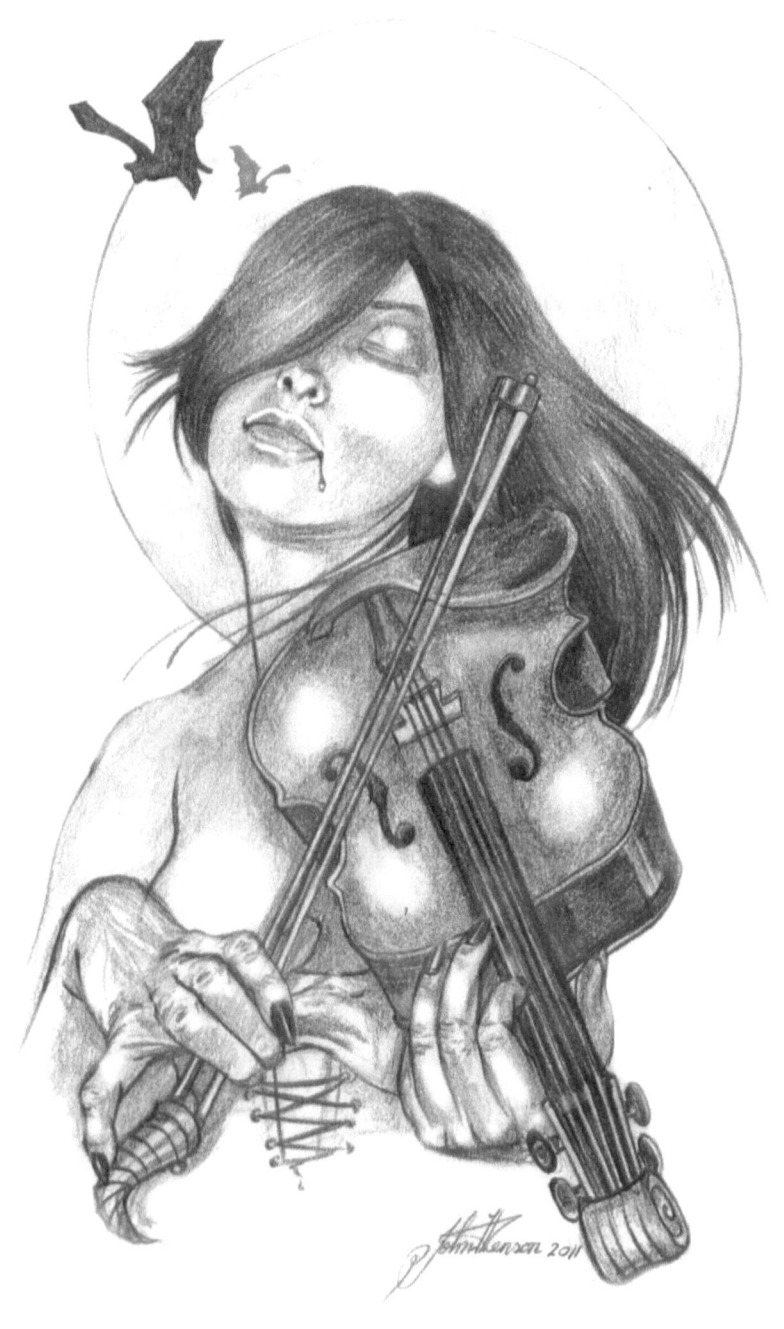

Night Music
Illustration for the poem 'Night Music

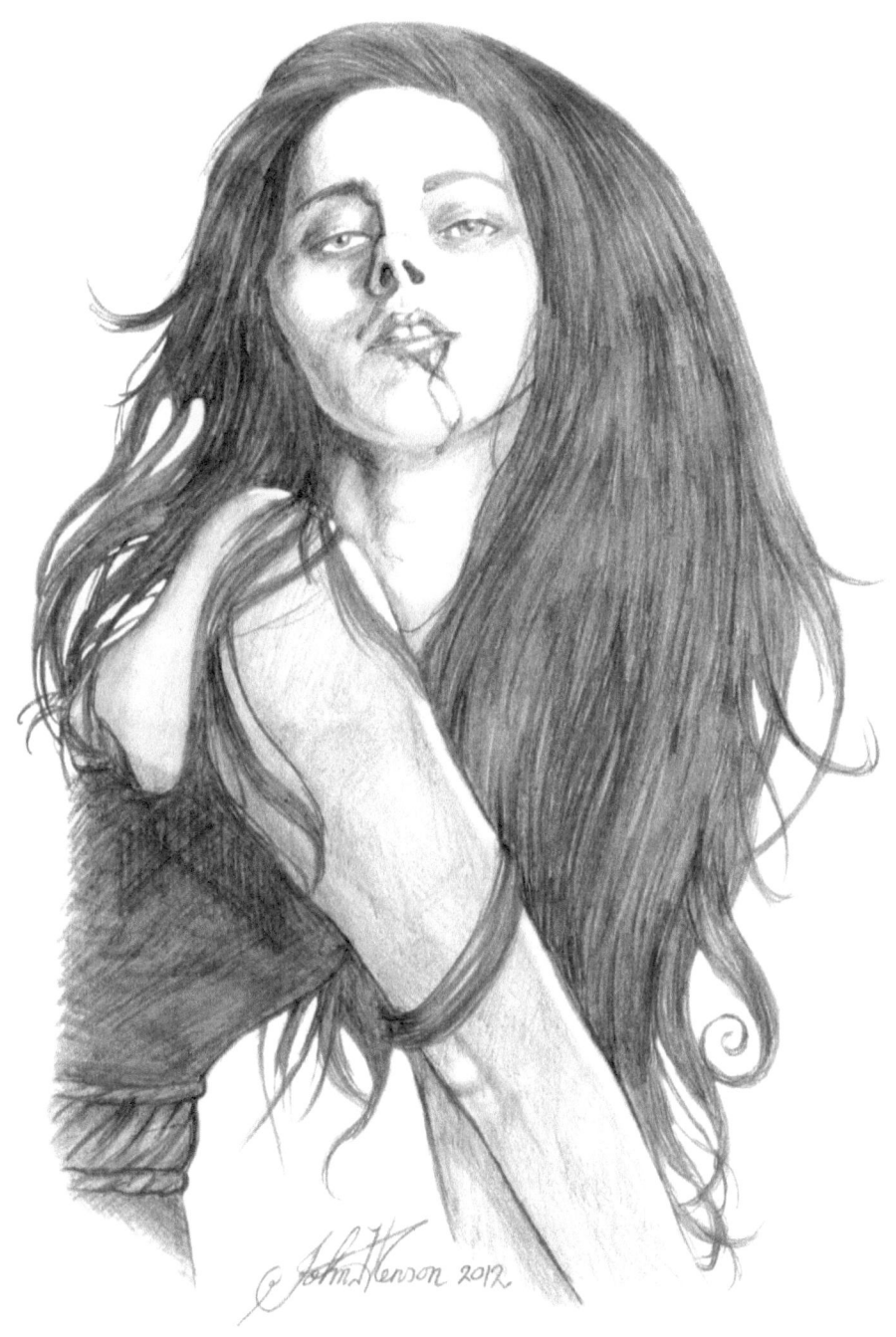

Clarissa

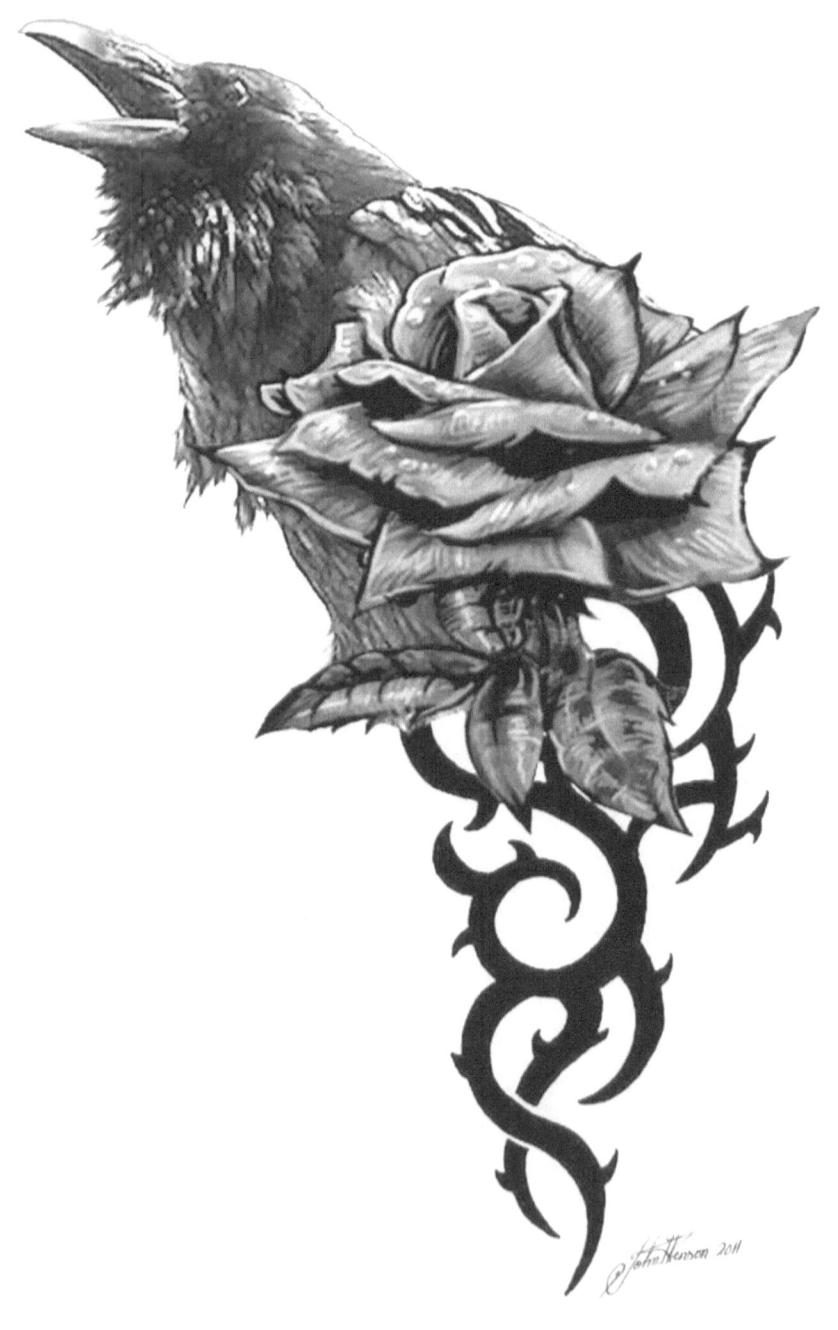

Raven and the Rose
Illustration for the cover of 'Darklingmire'

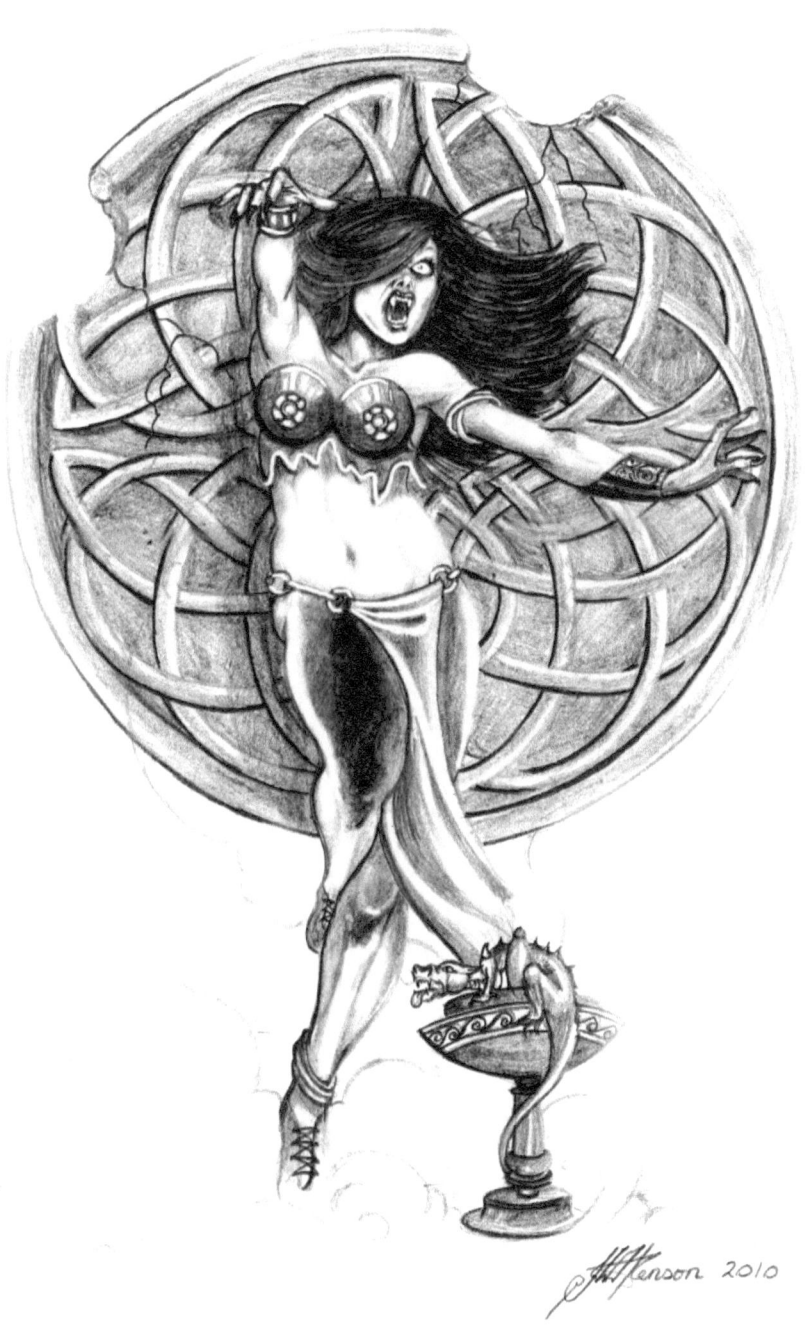

Fasgadair
Ancient Celtic vampire

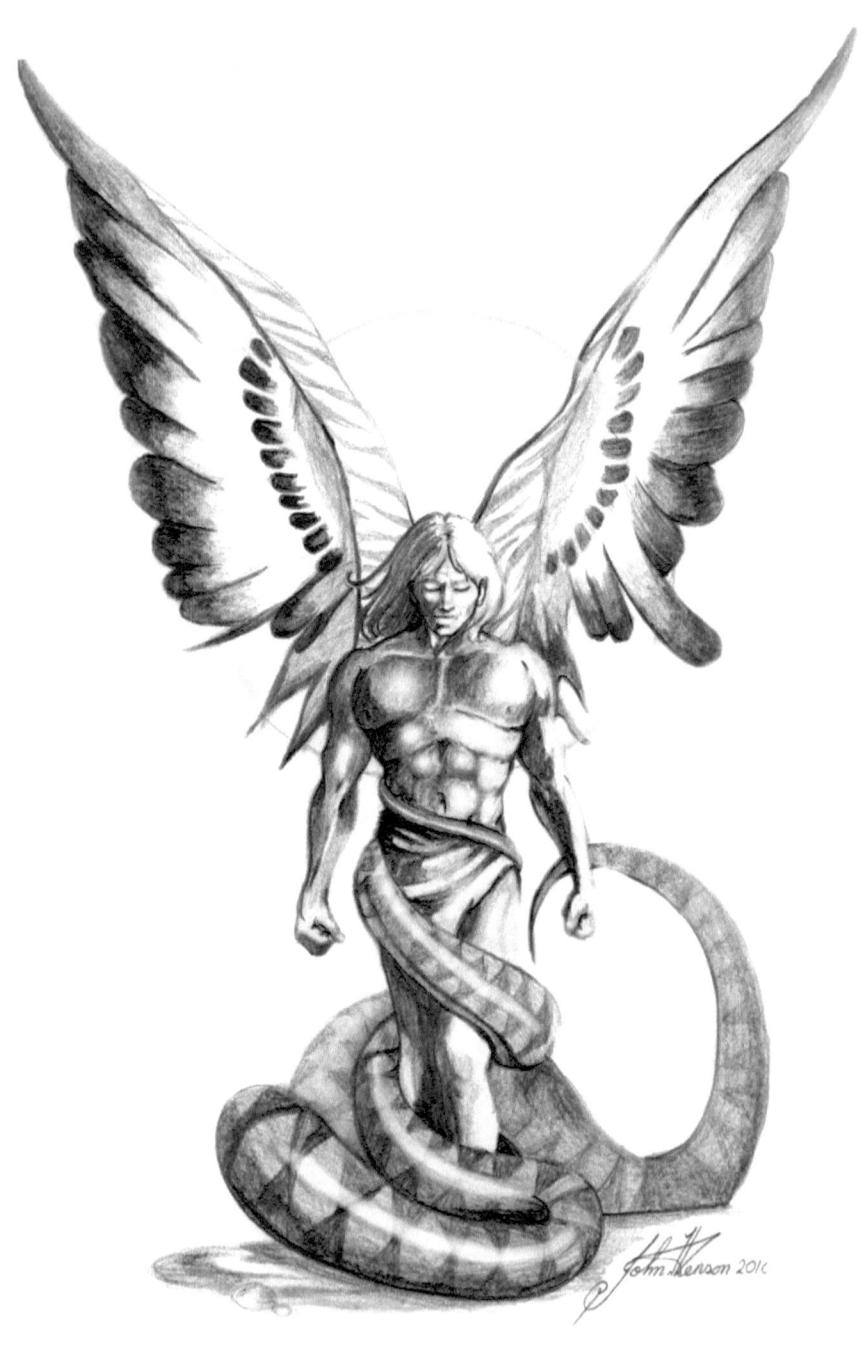

The Angel and the Serpent

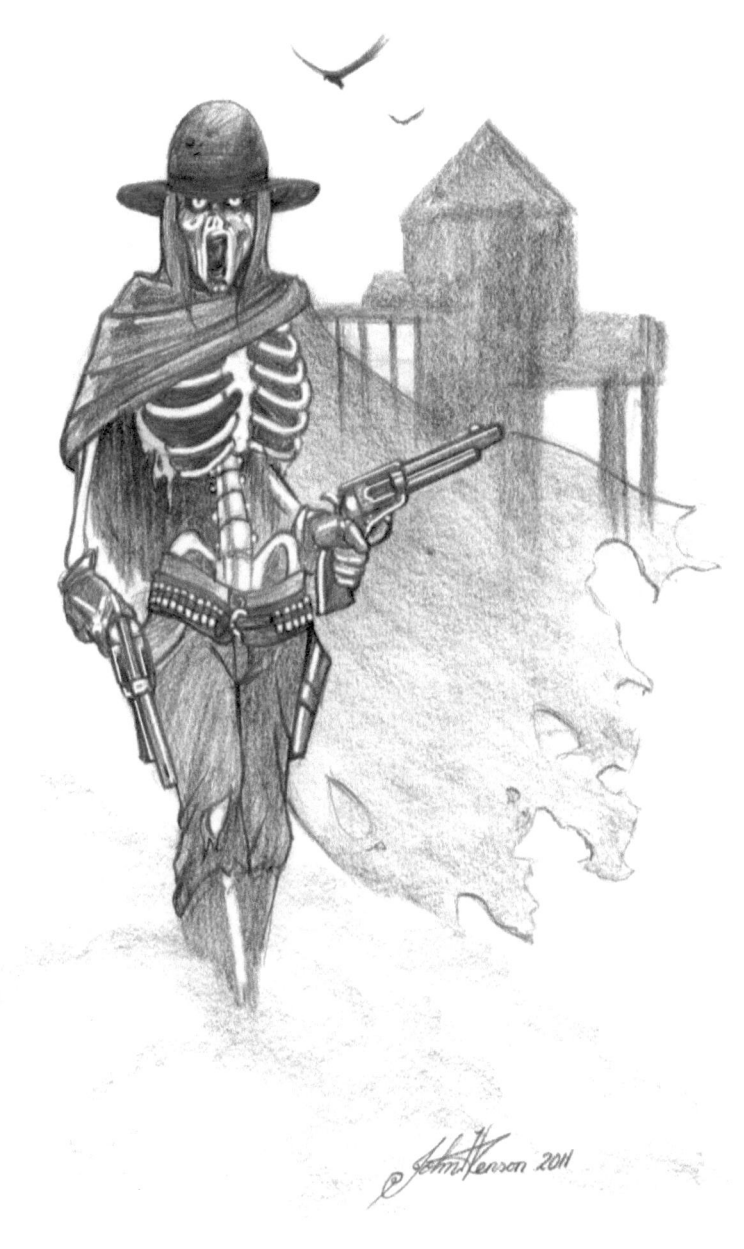

Ghost Town

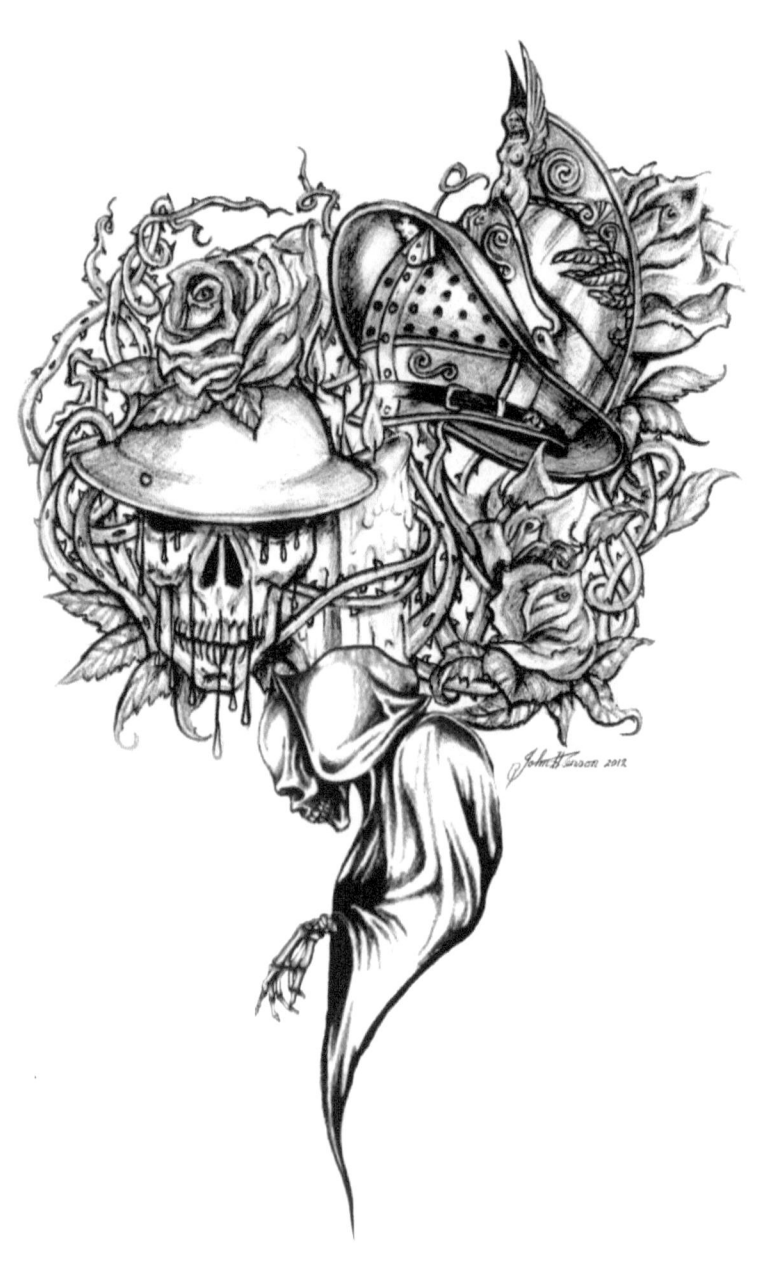

War
The symbols of conflict and its results

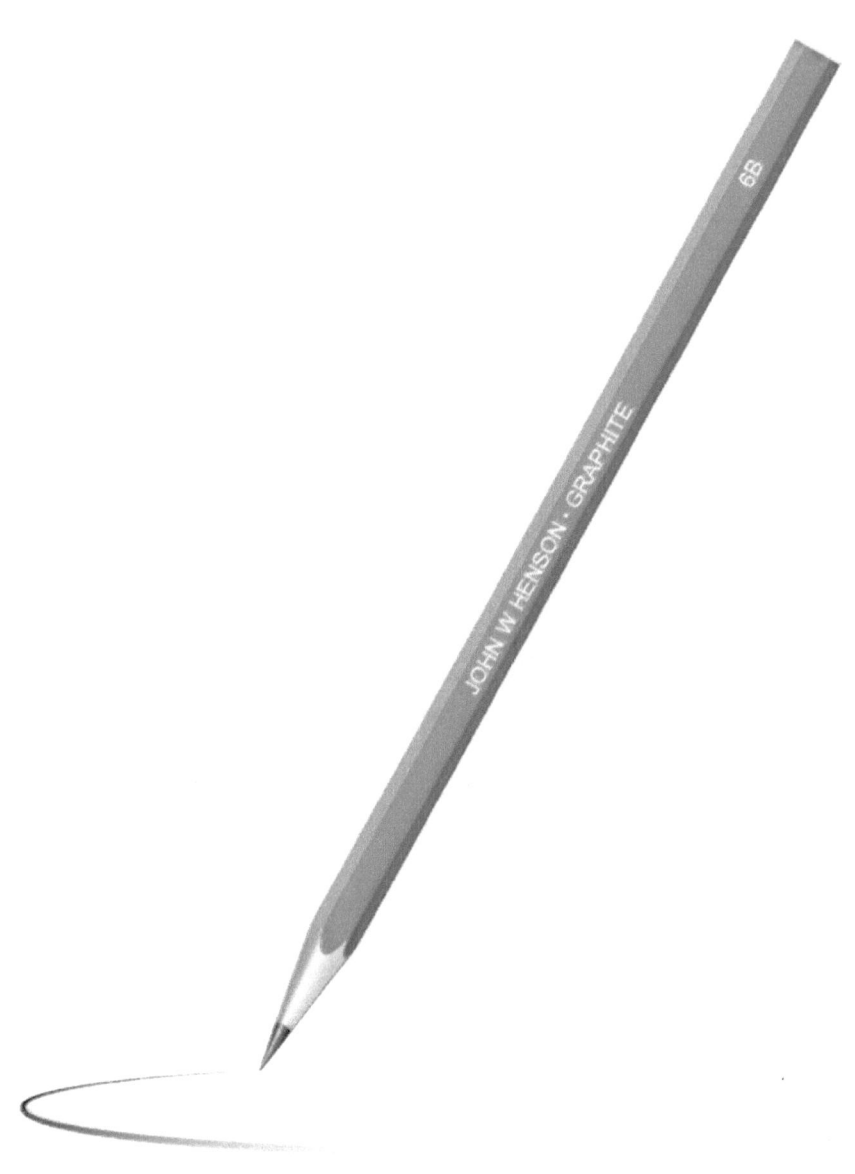

Cartoons

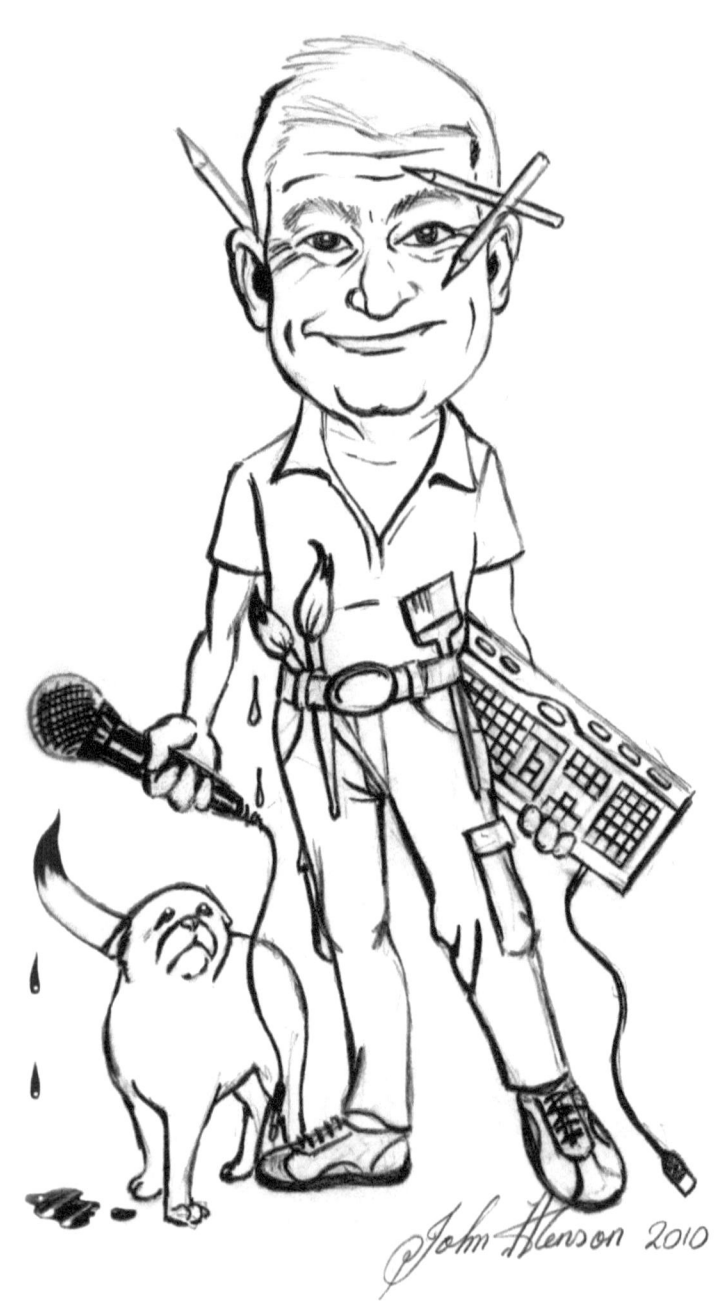

Me Toon
Trying to do everything at once

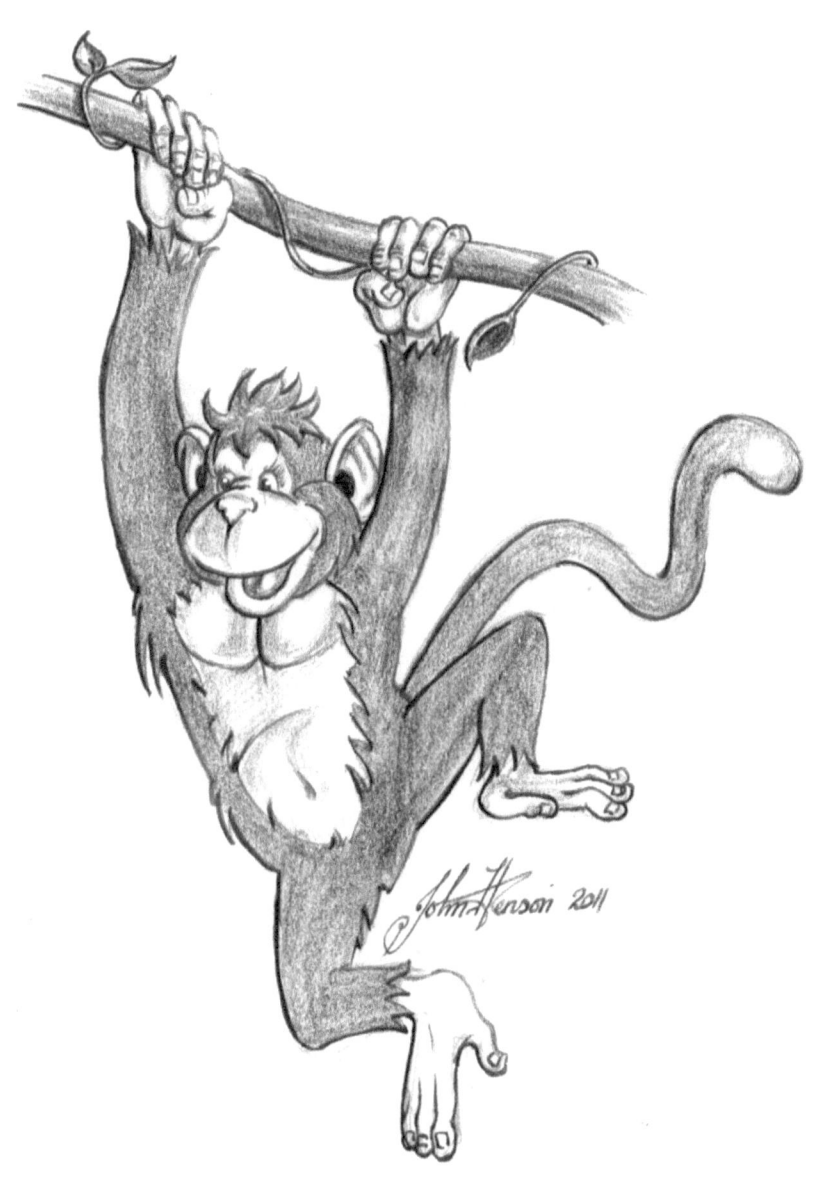

Cheeky Monkey

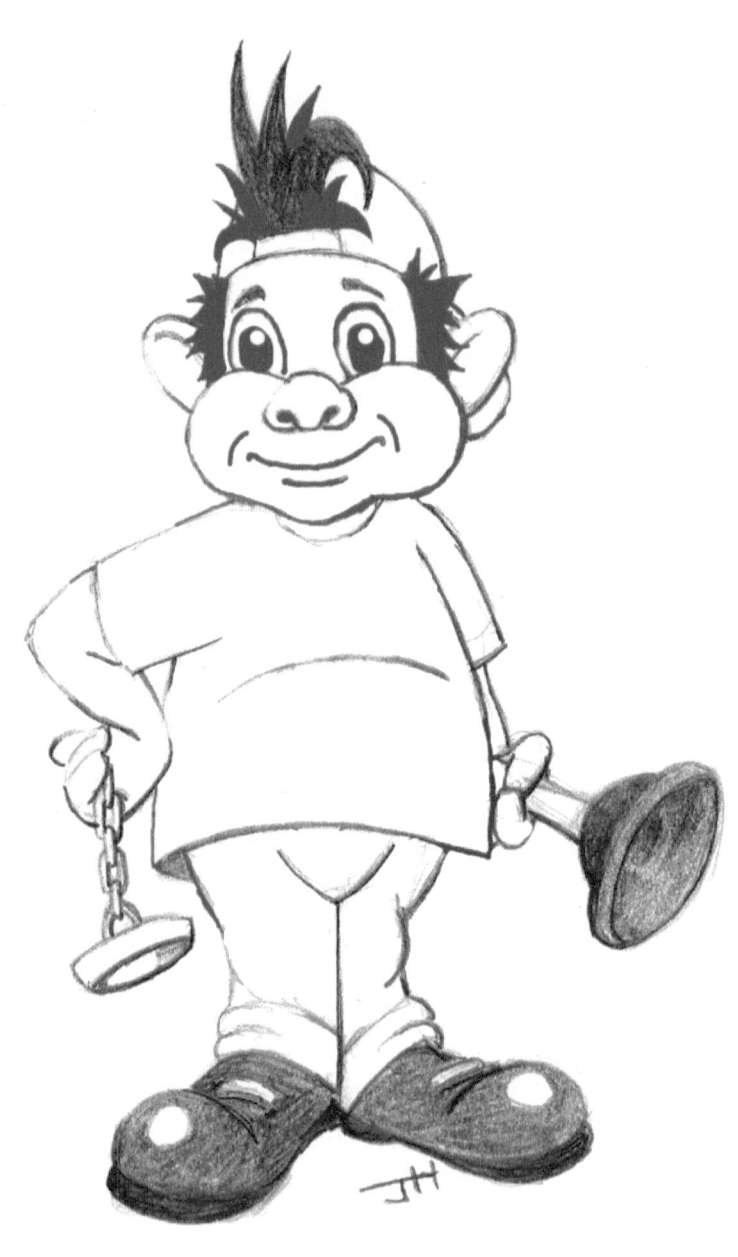

Pete the Plumber

Character for a plumbing company

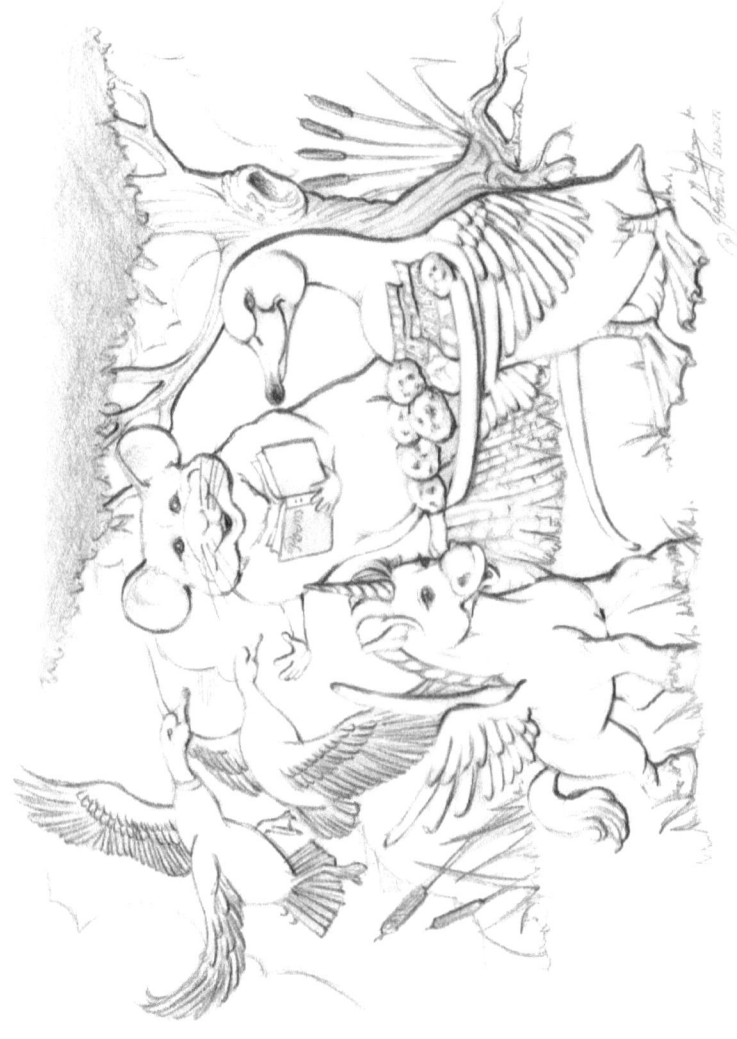

An Impromptu Poetry Recital
Inspired by my daughter and her friends

57

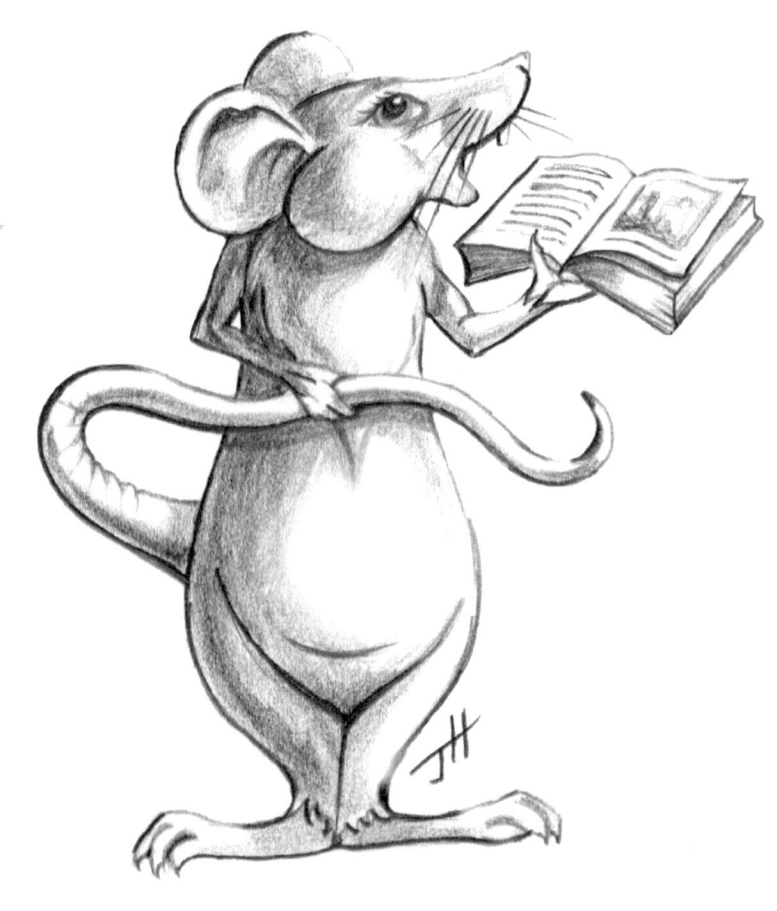

A Literate Mouse

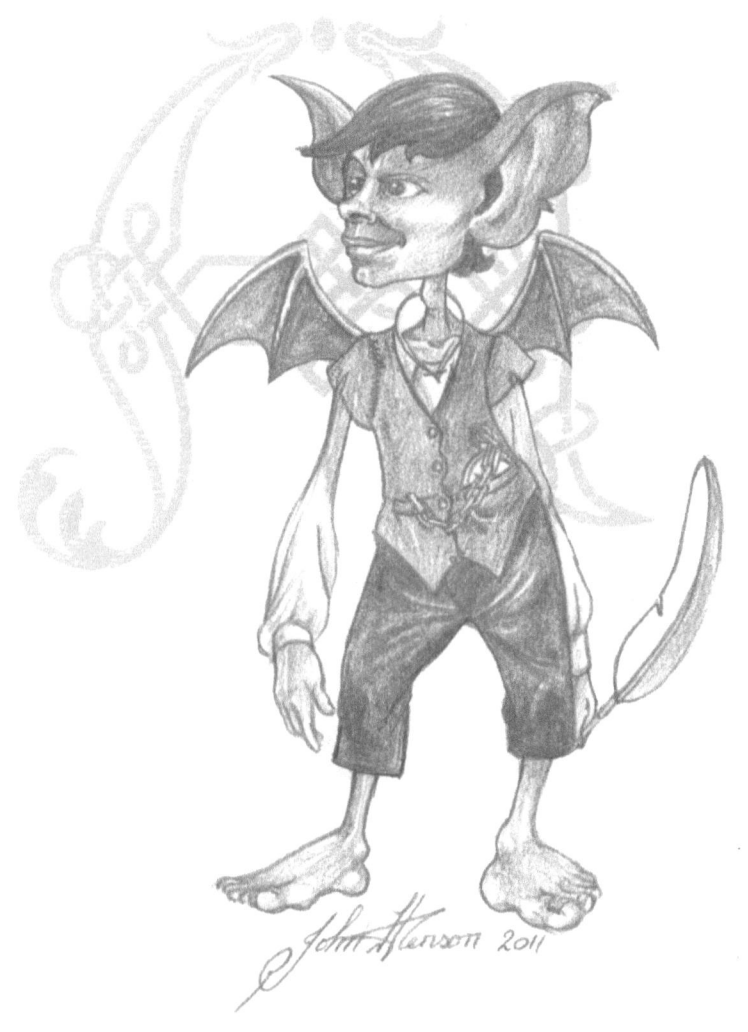

Horatio Tinkle

Illustration for 'Horatio Tinkle and the Quill of Oroboros'

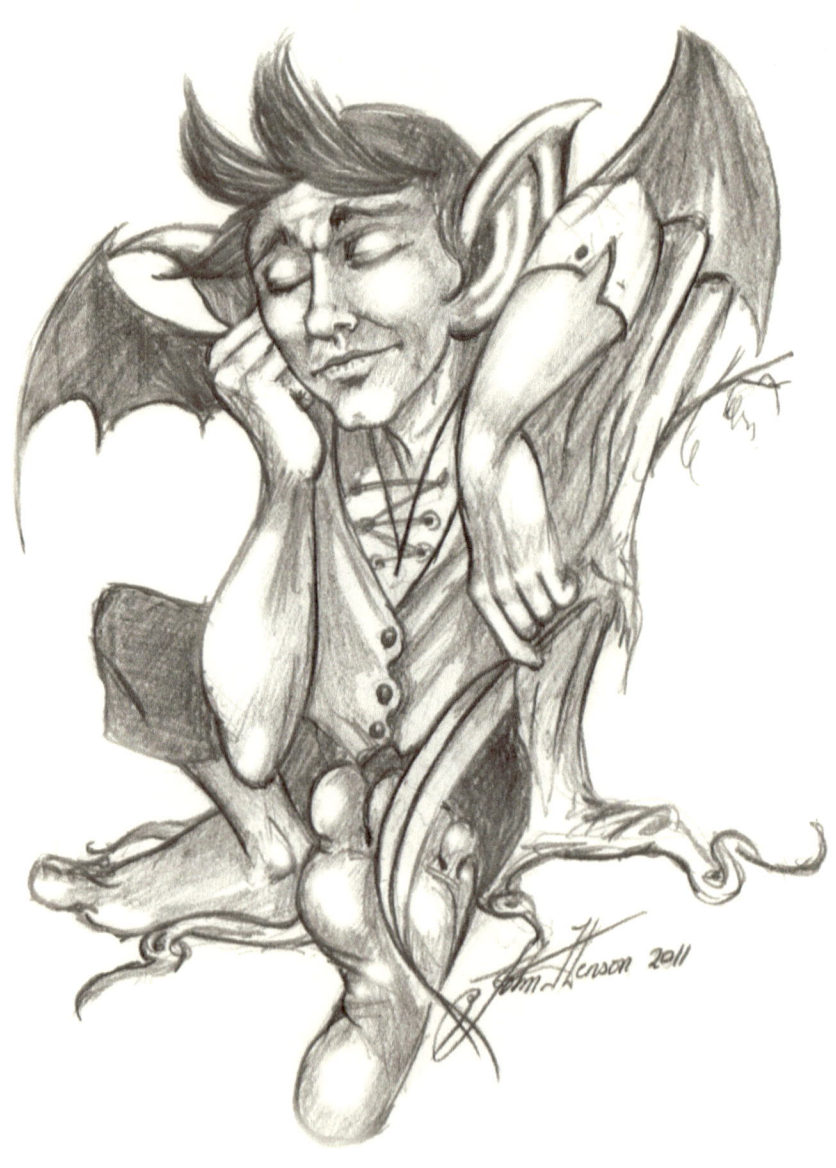

Fruitbat Dreams
Ignatious Tinkle for the poem 'Give and Take

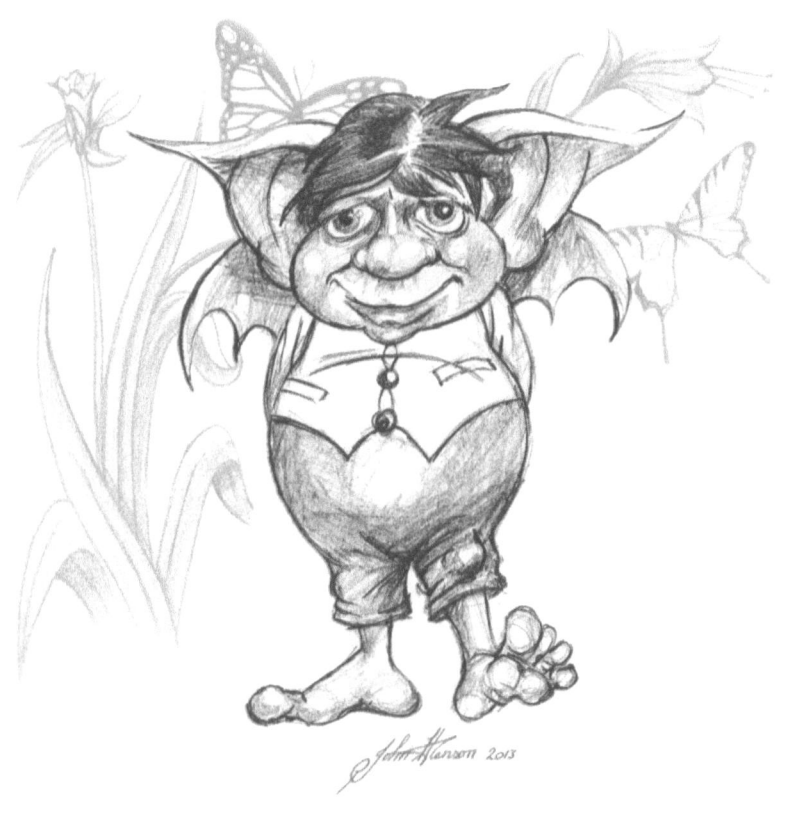

Lumpkin Plod

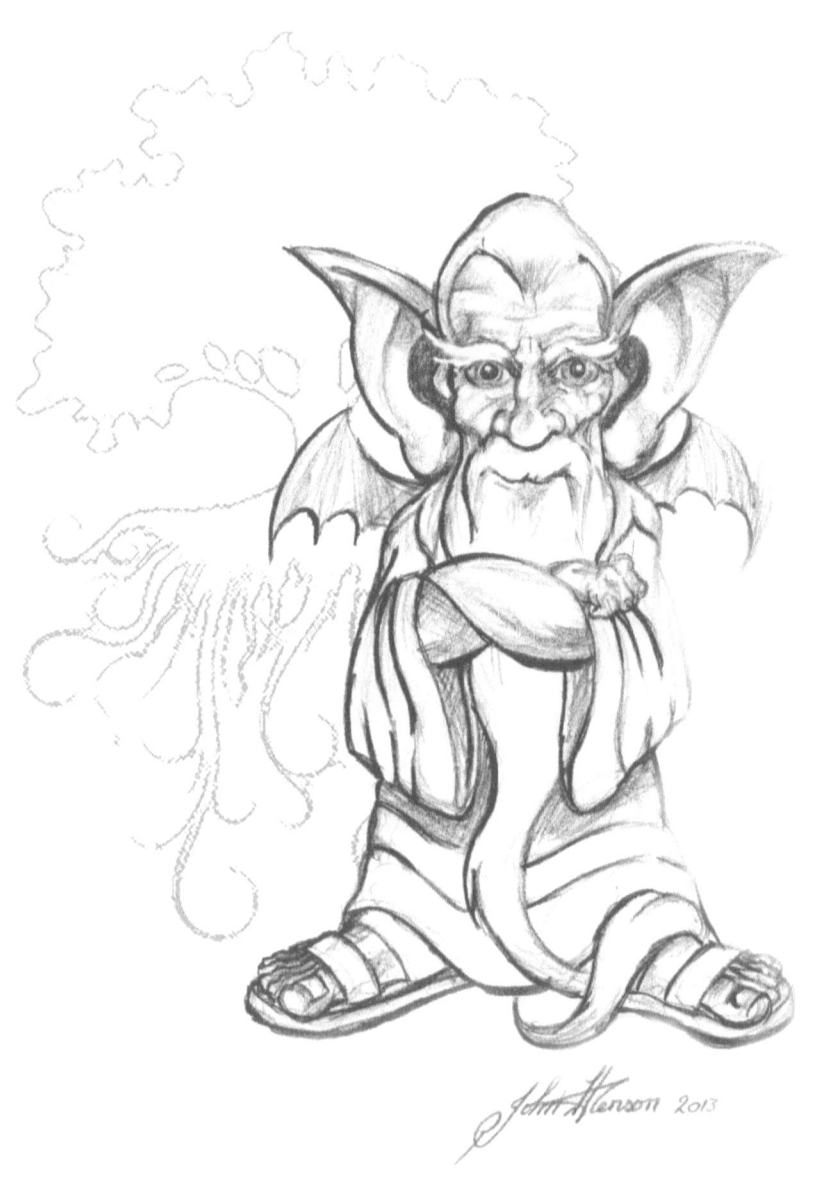

Mugwort the Mage

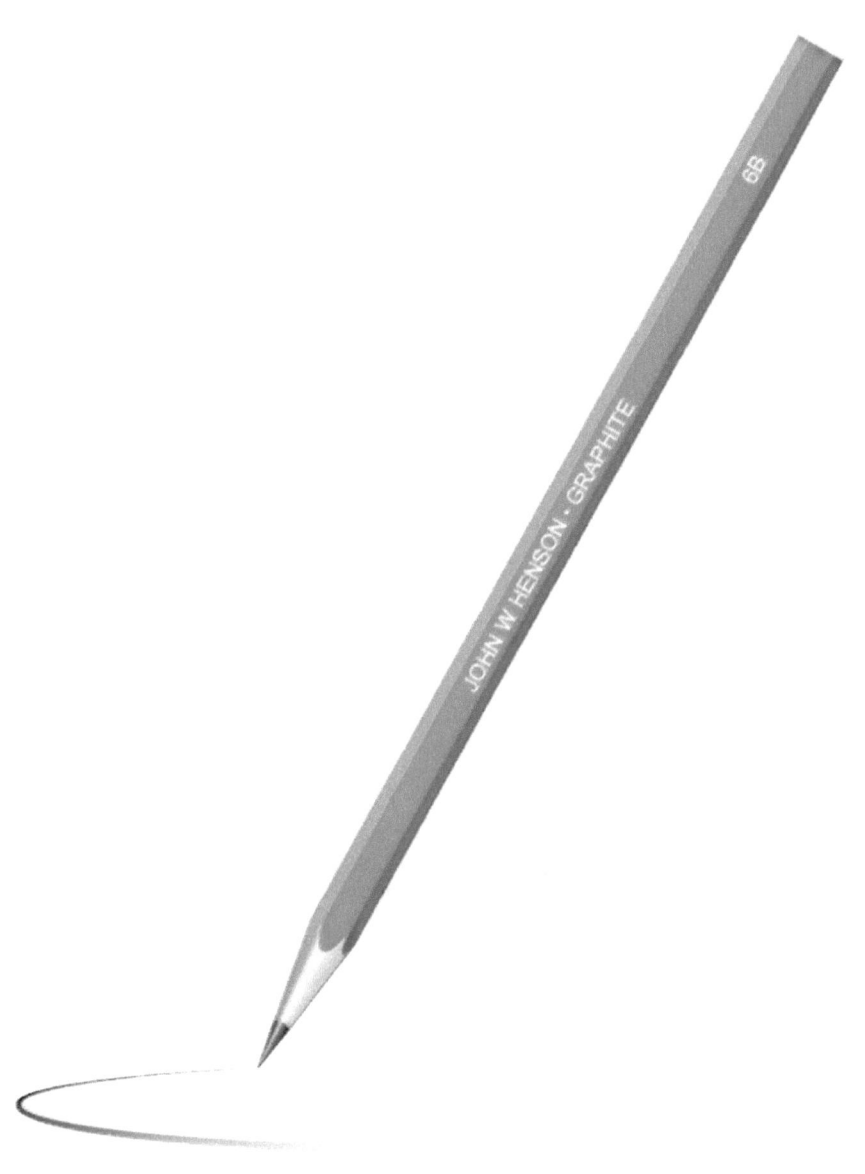

Miscellaneous

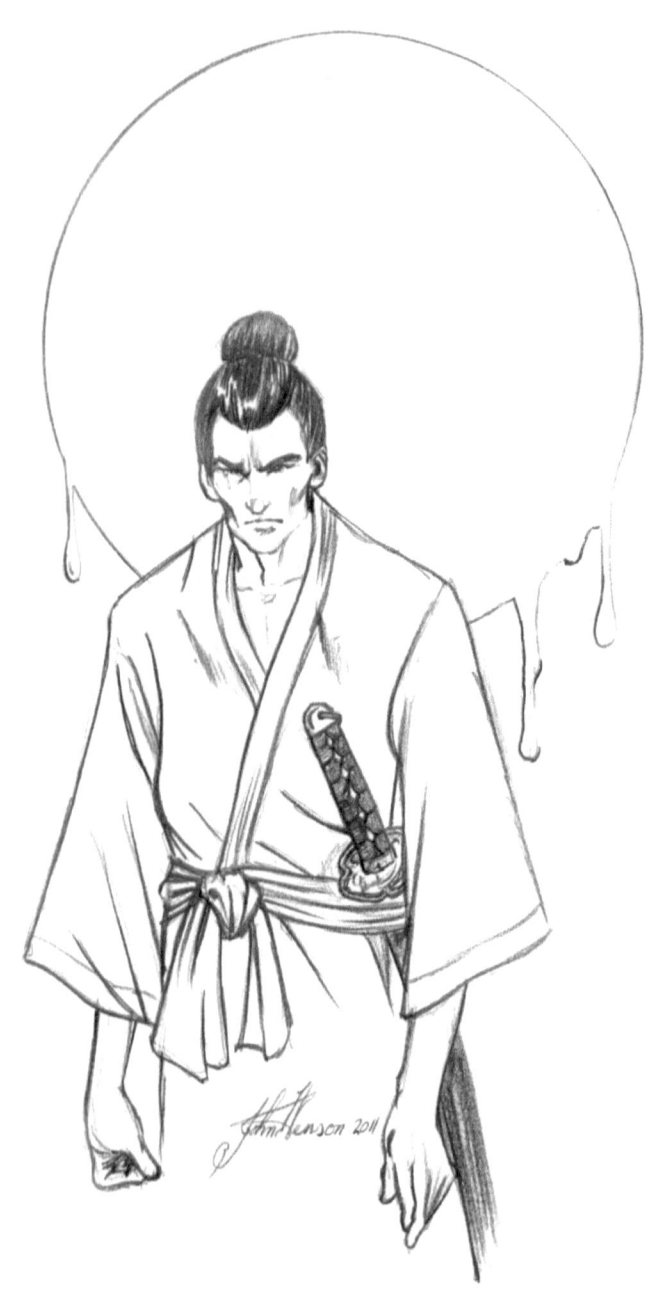

Tears of the Sun
For Japanese Tsunami Charity book

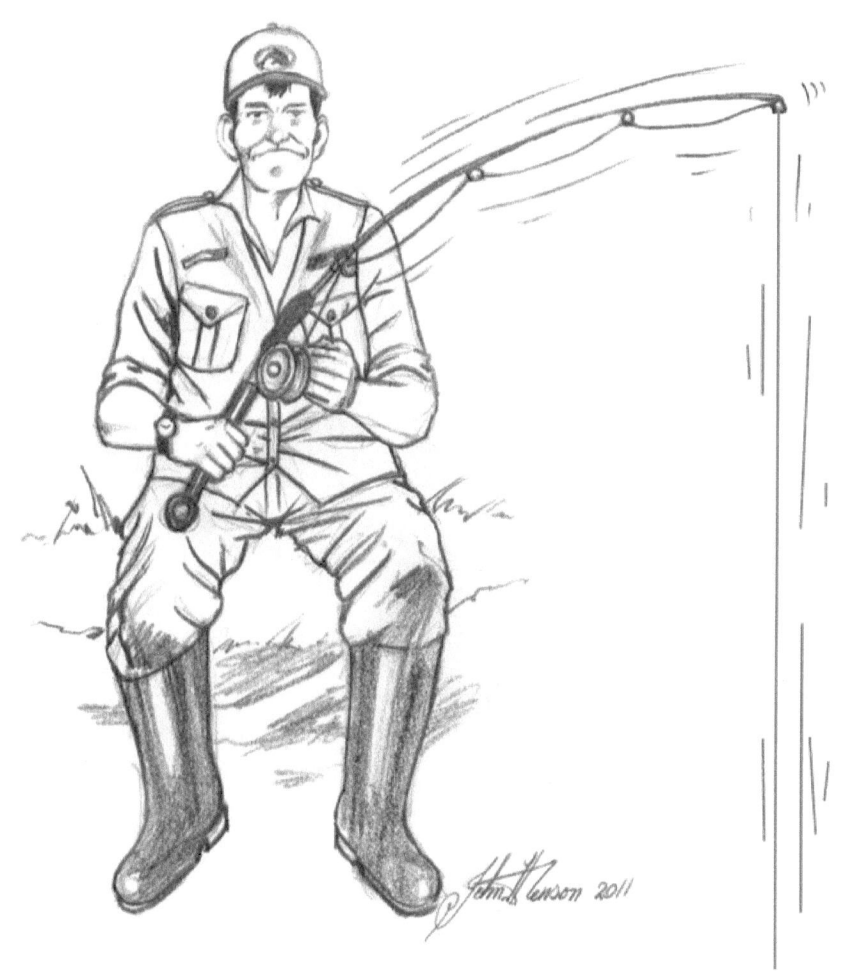

On the Line

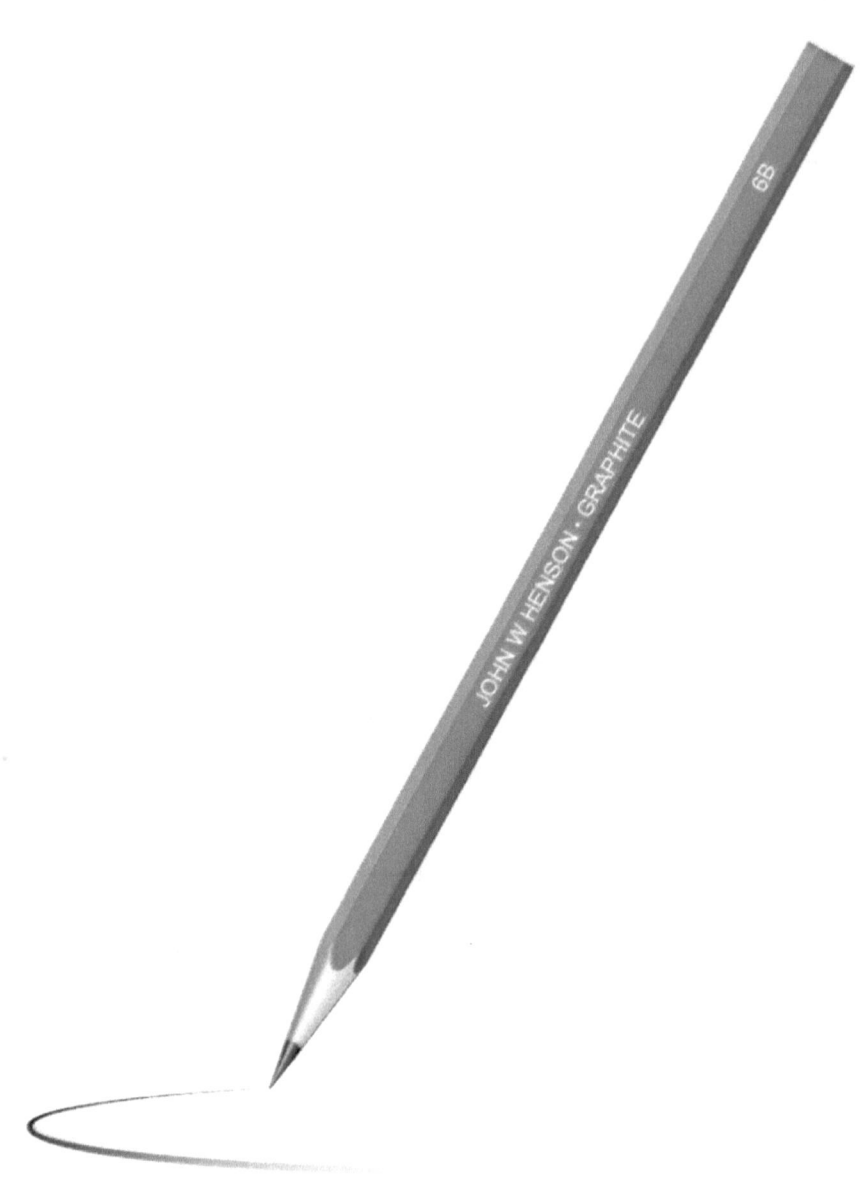

The Chronicles of Gildas
Illustrations for the book

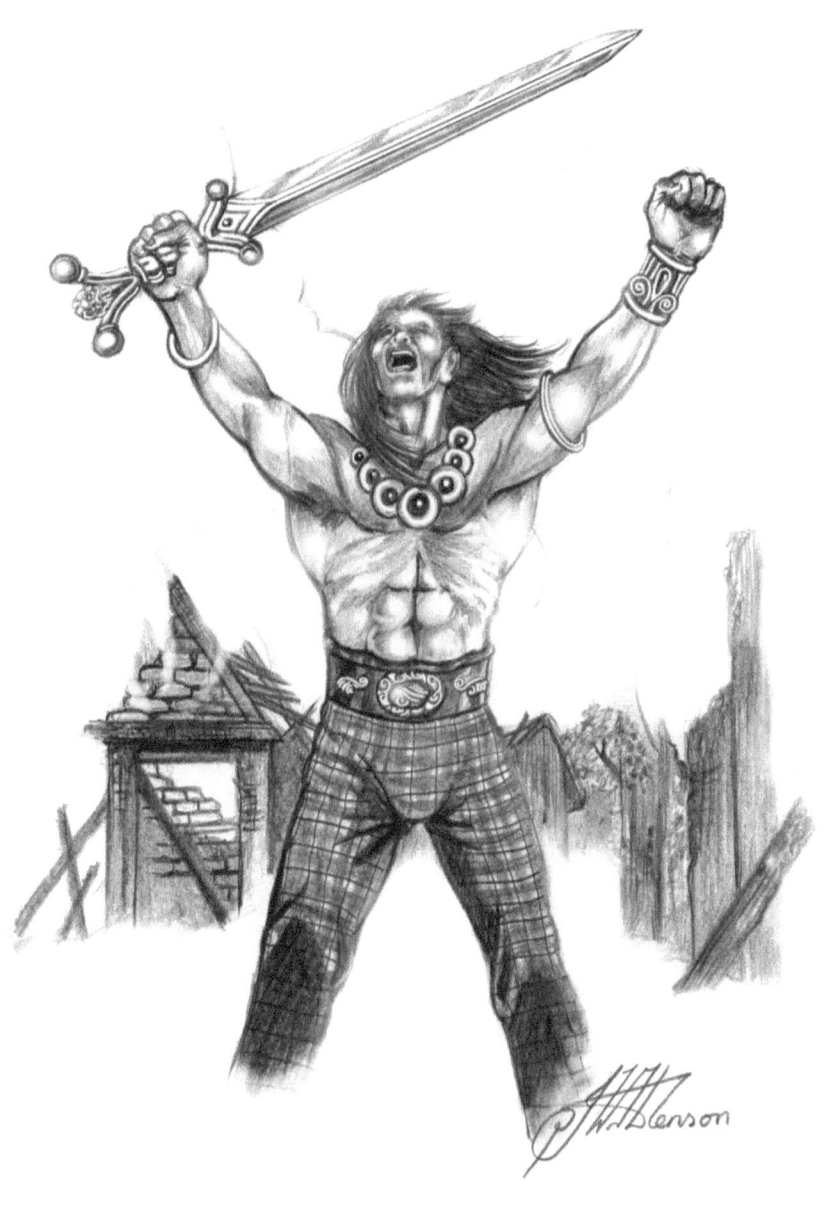

The Parting

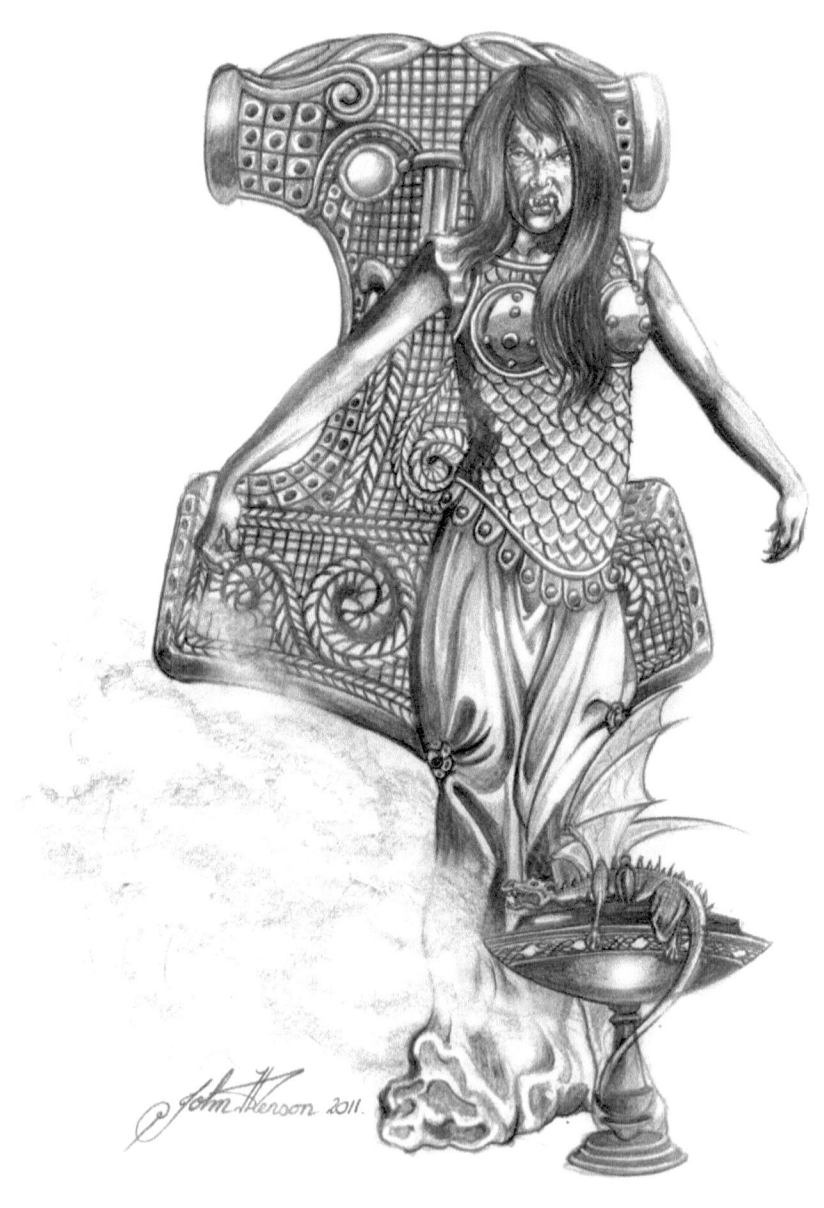

Into the Dark

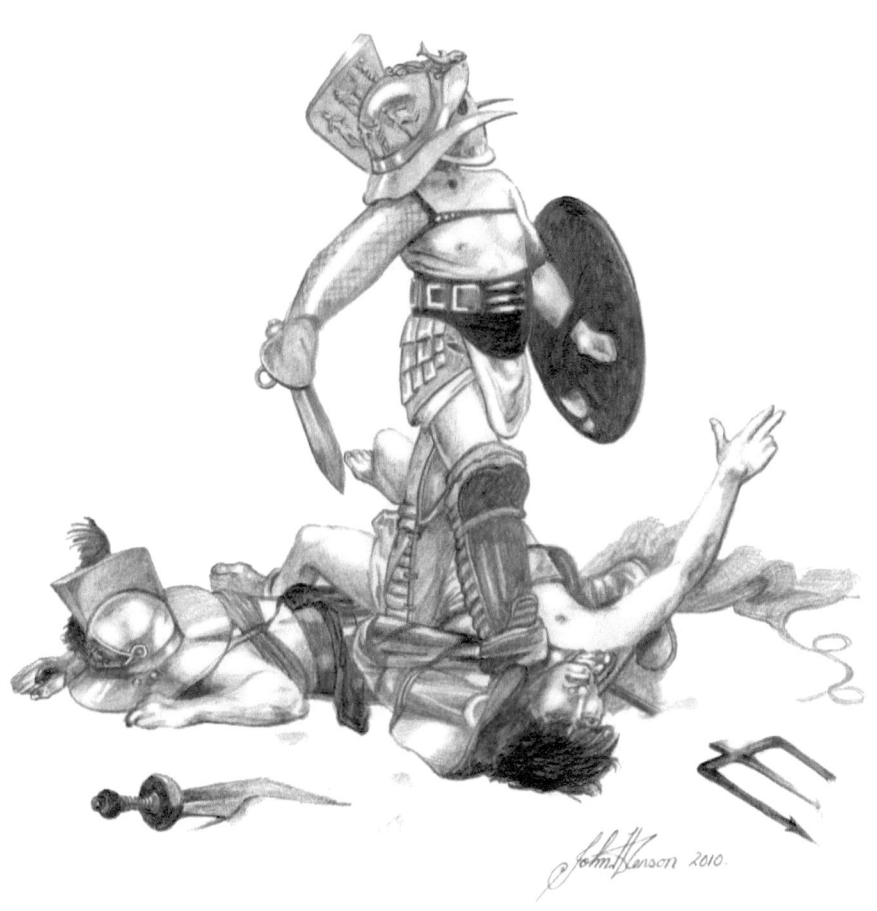

Ave Morituri Te Salutant

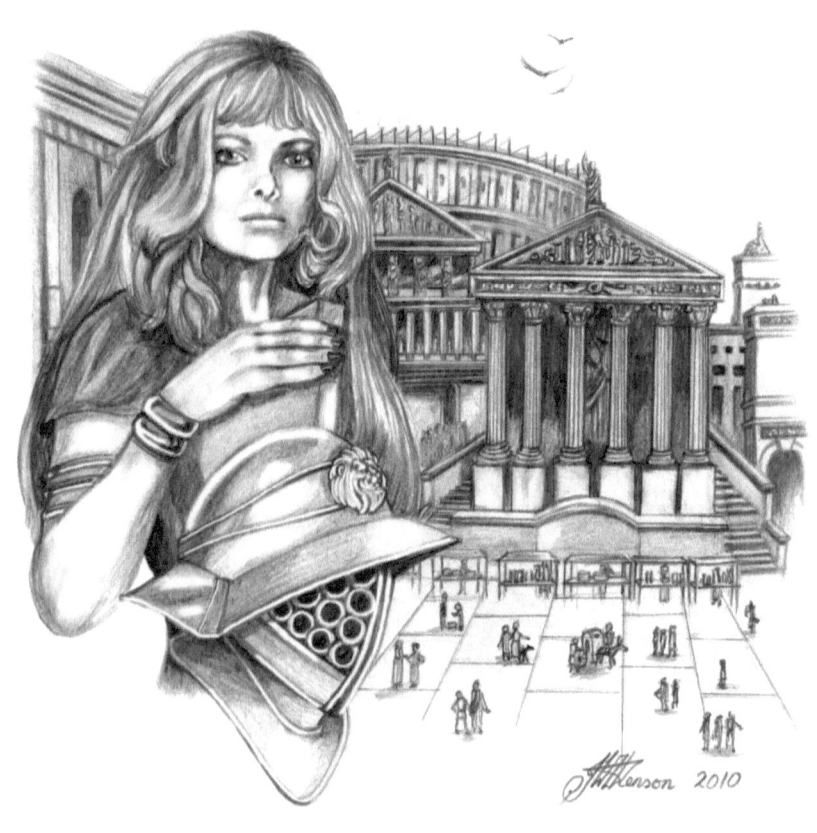

Senatus Populusque Romanus

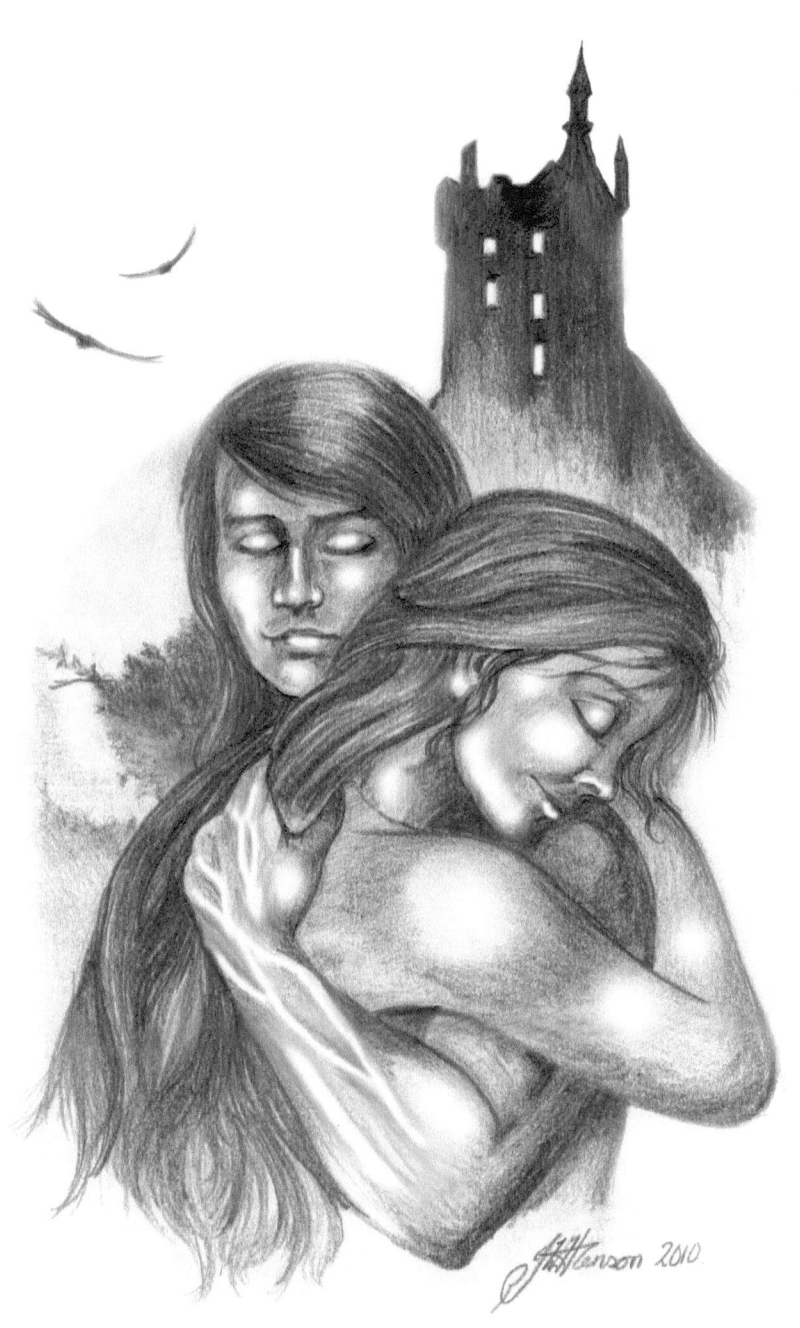

Chivalry and Betrayal

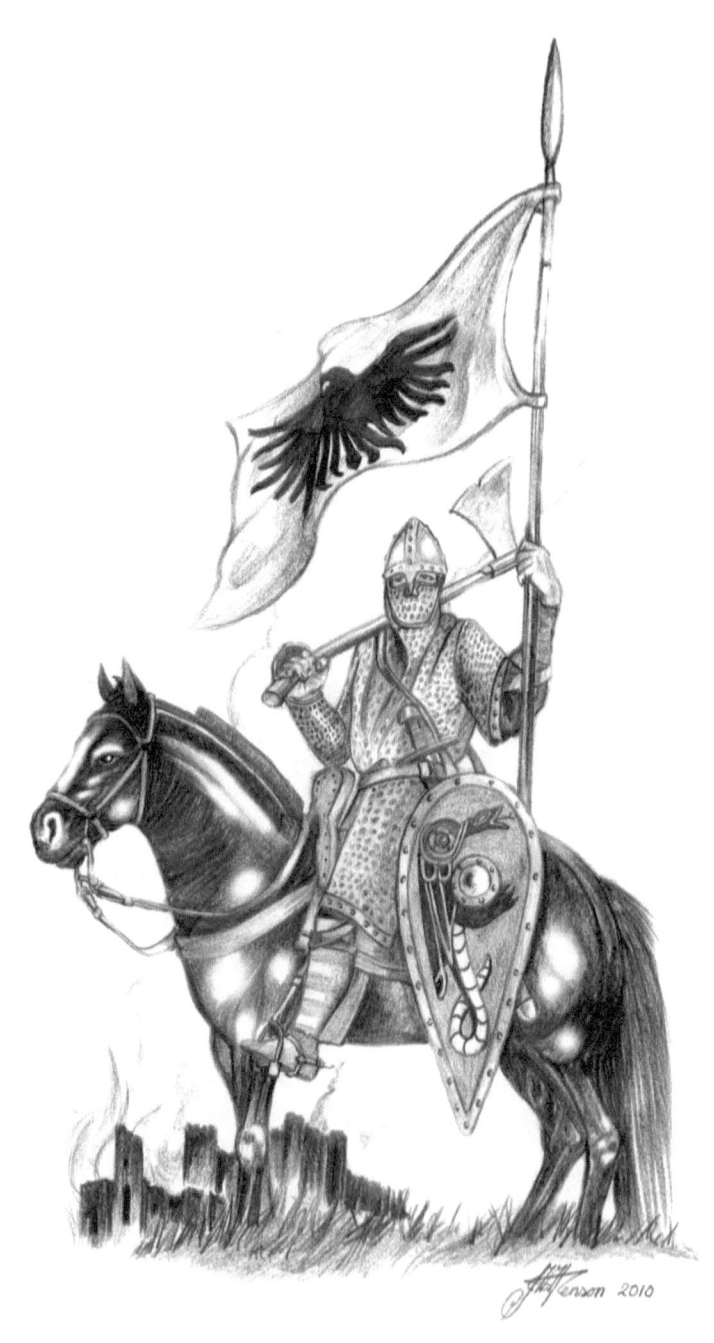

The Raven's Dream

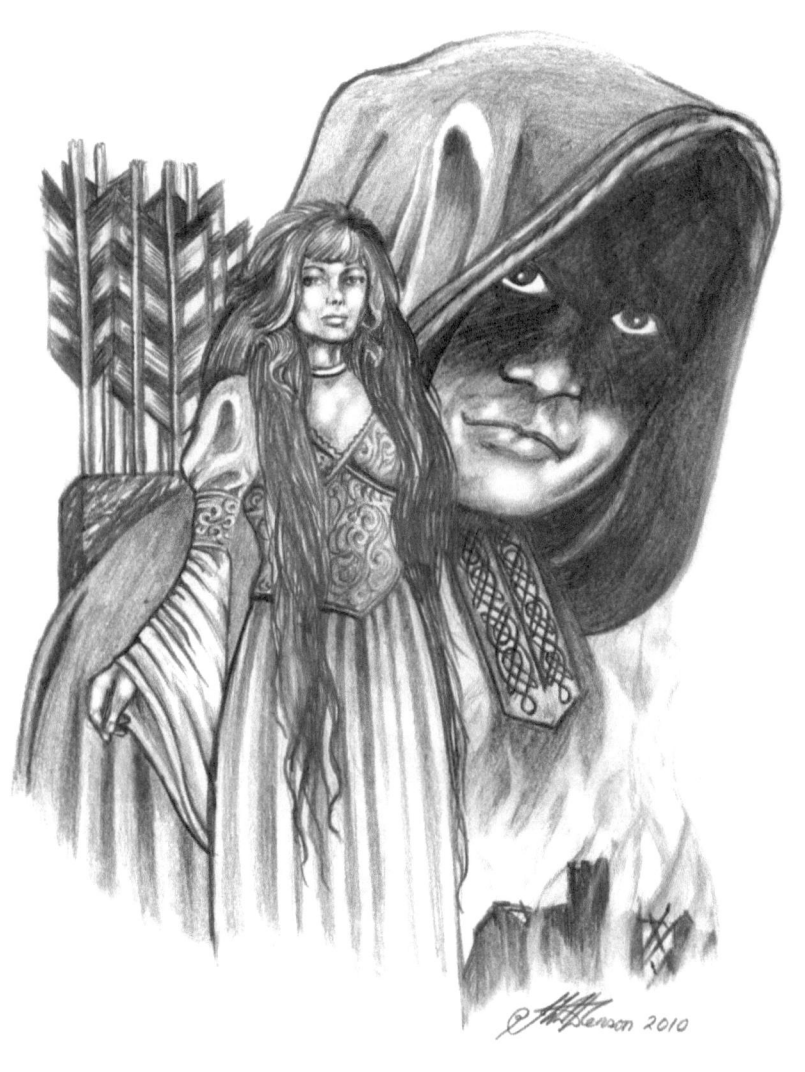

Heart Arrow

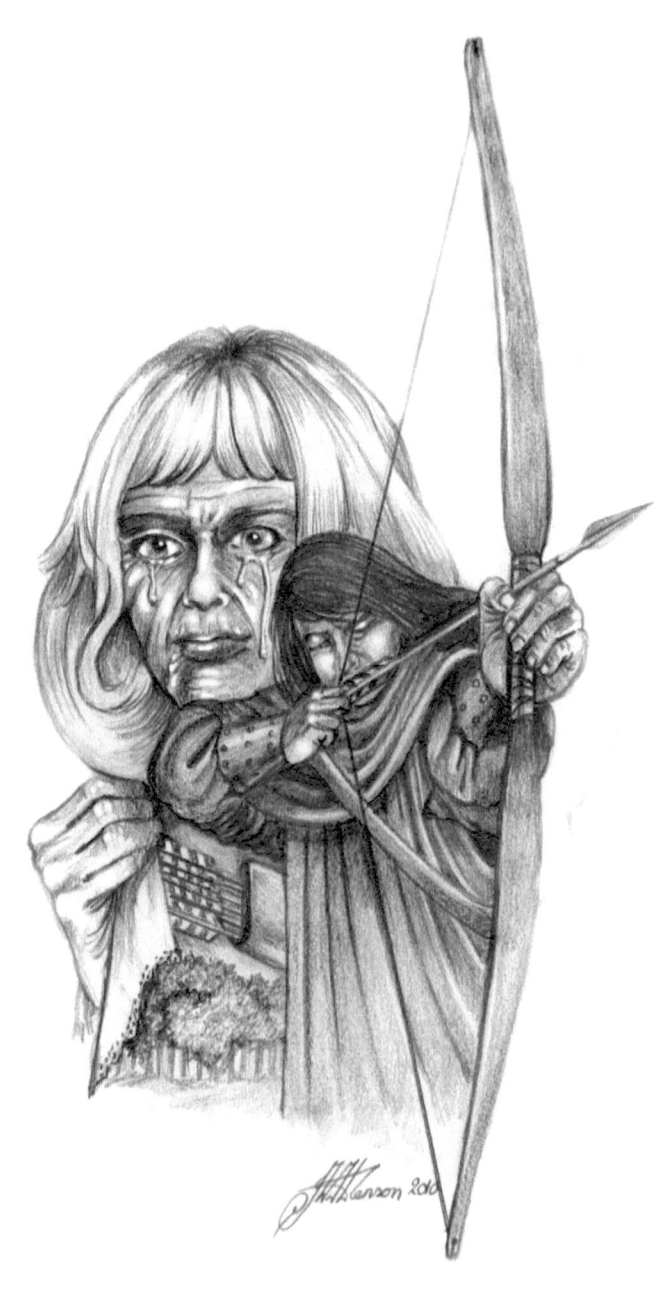

The Arrow's Mark

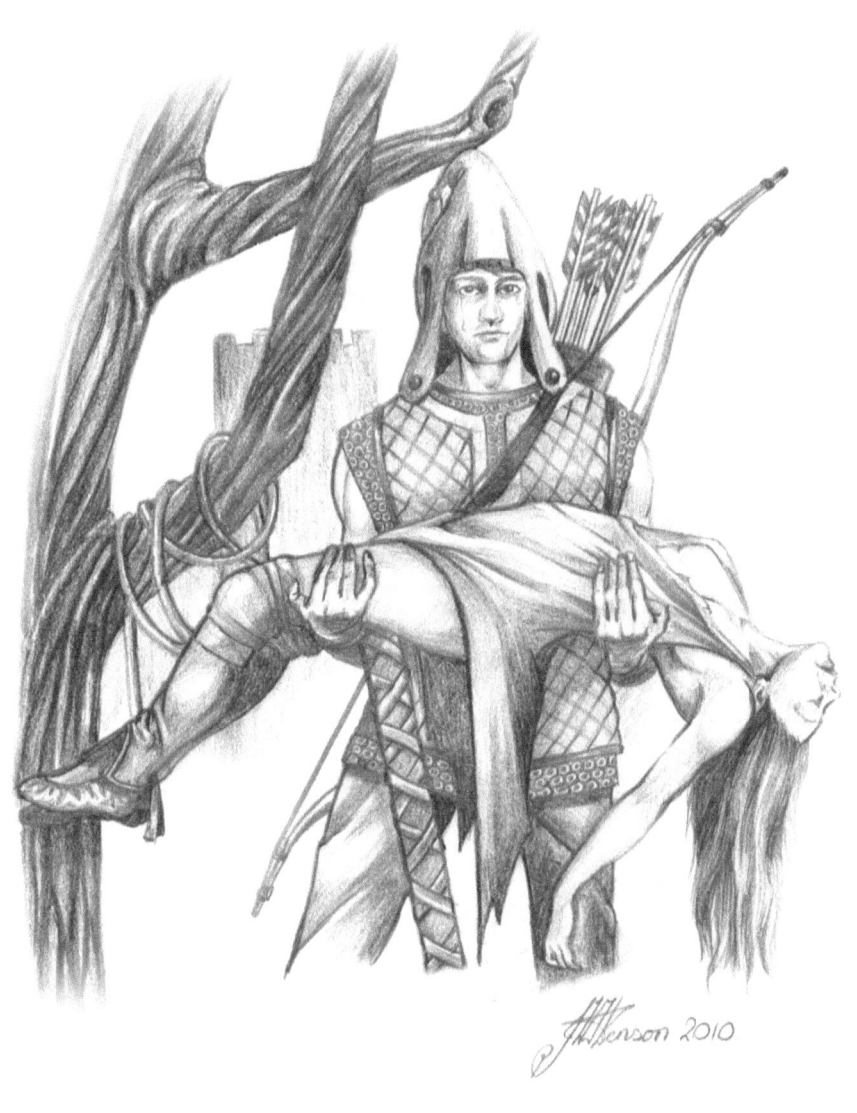

A Ring of Roses

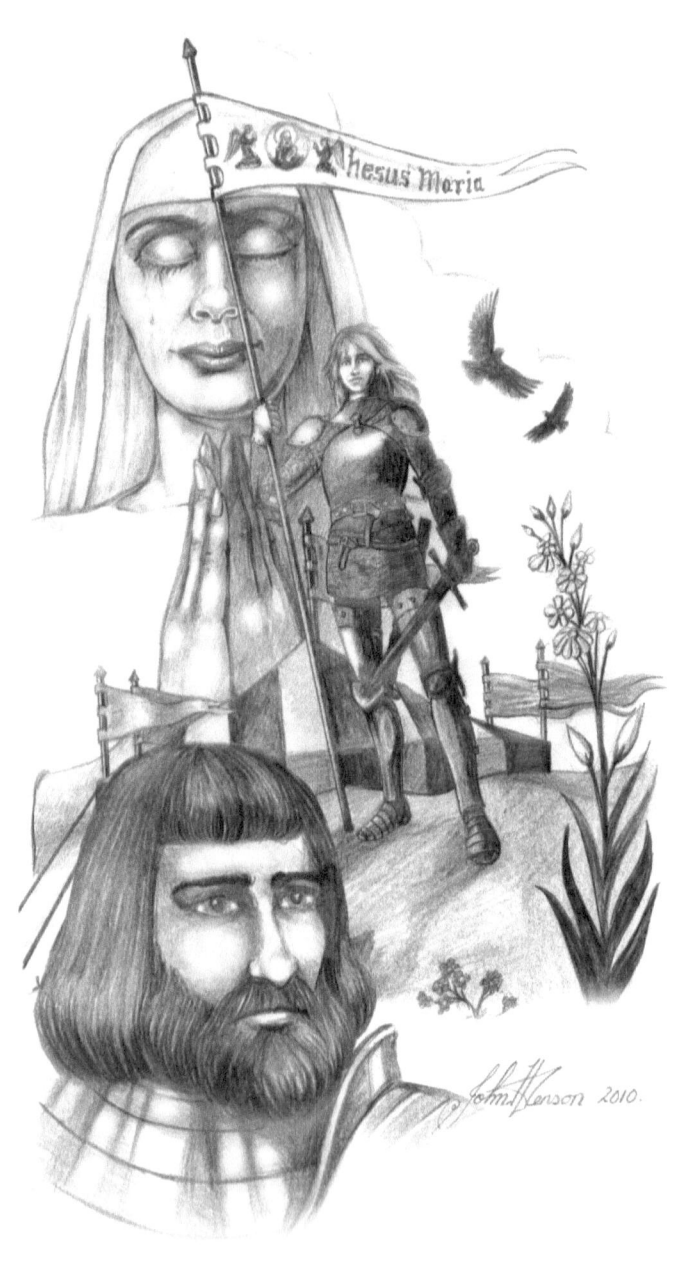

The Sword of God

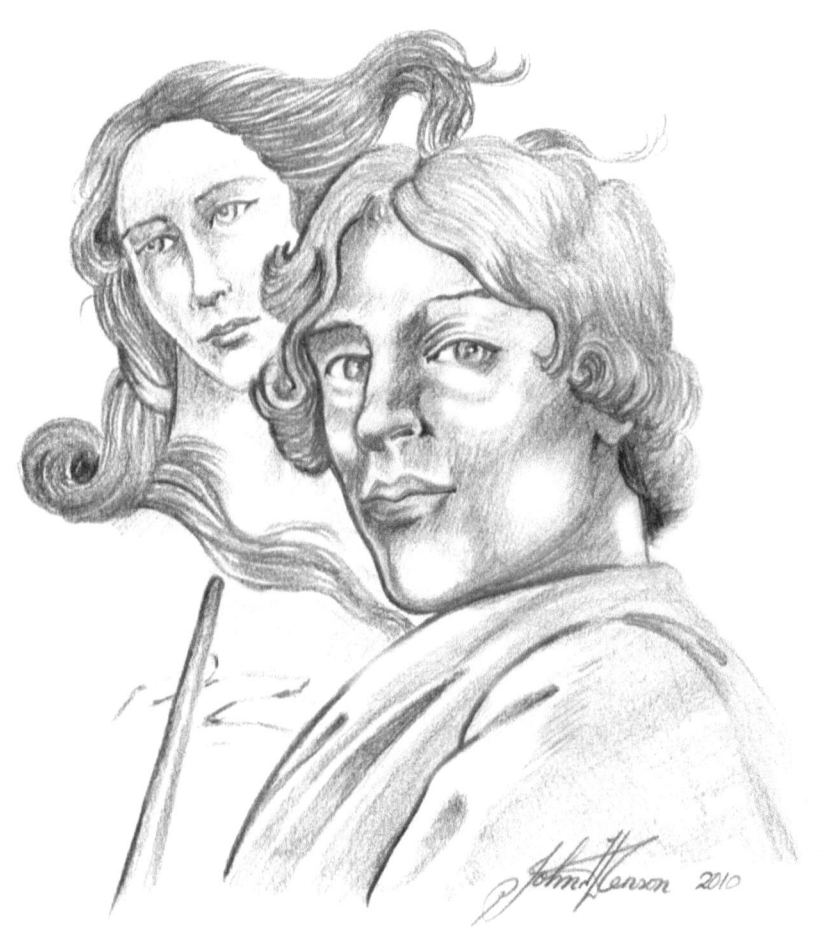

The Devil's Reign

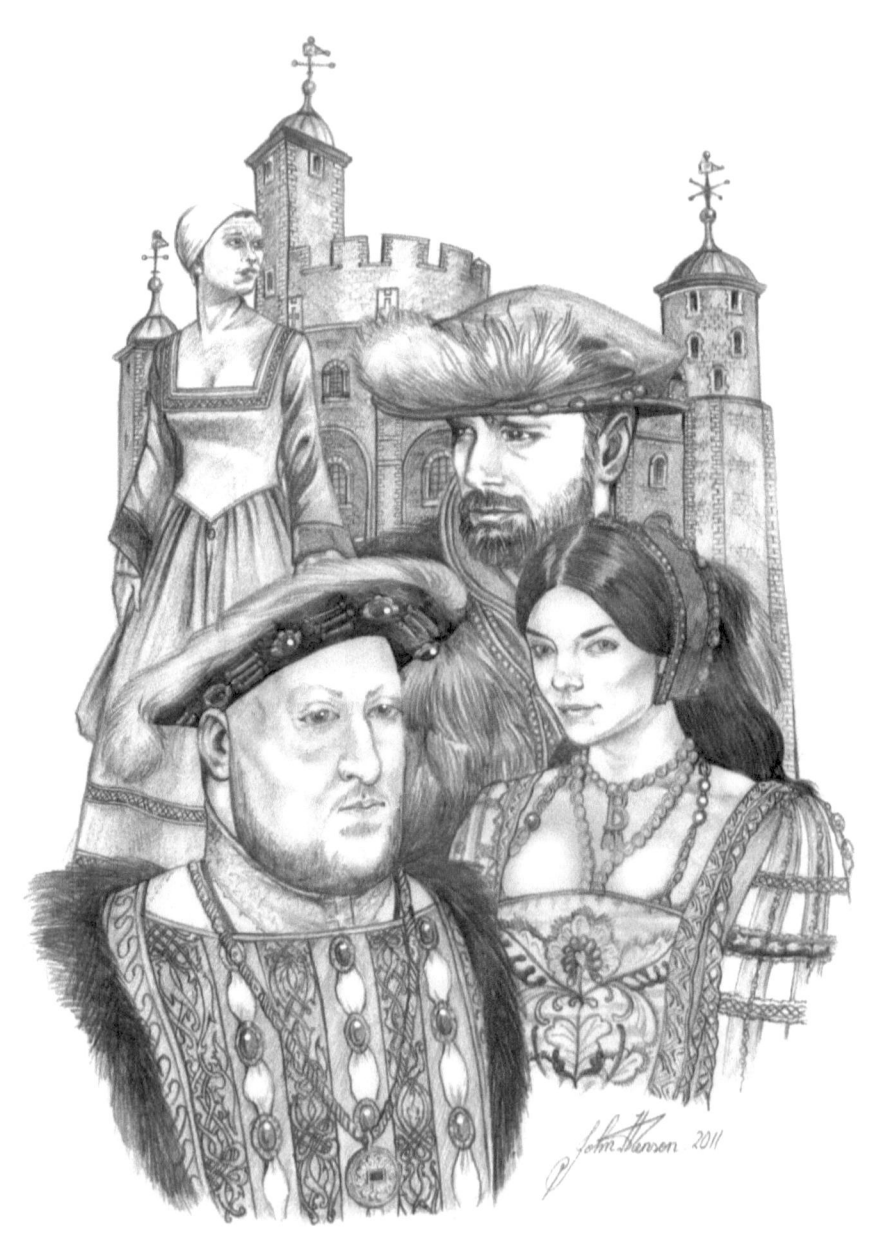

The Demon King

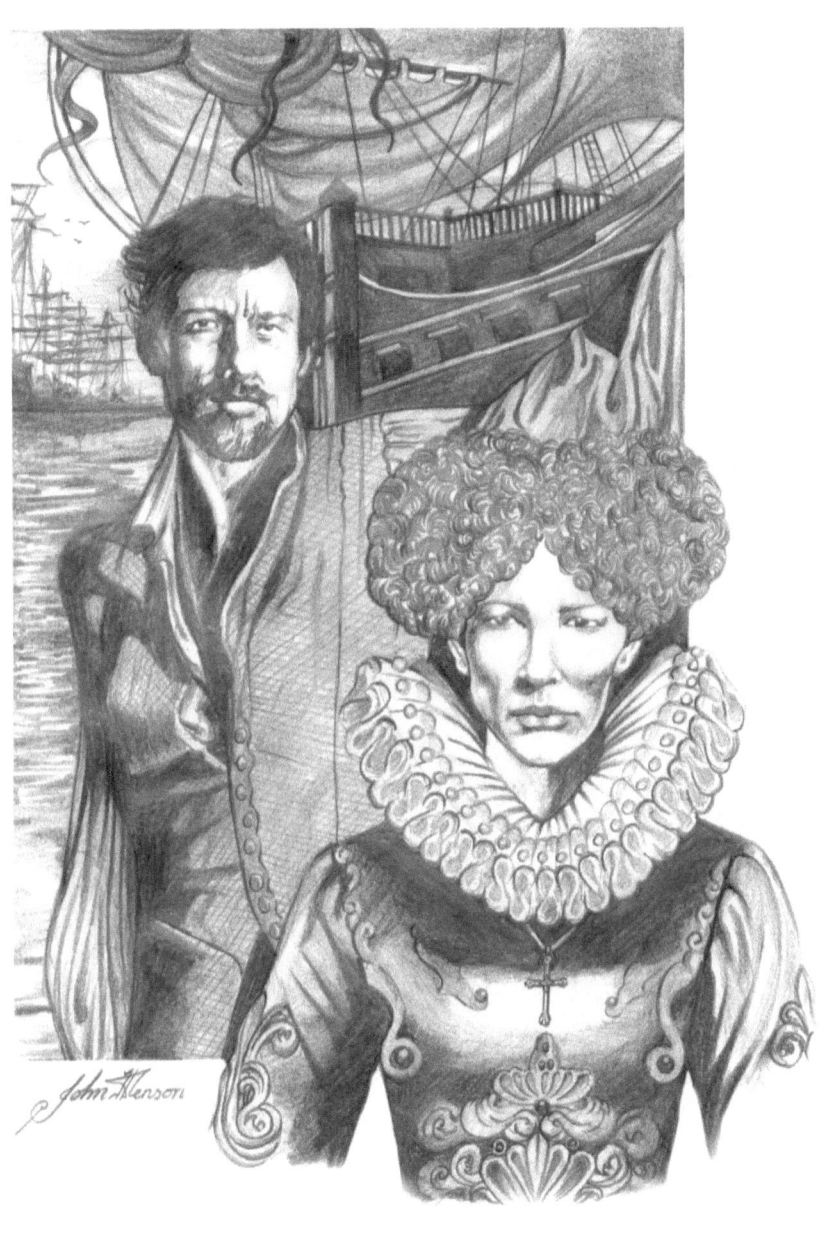

Regina Virgo Intacta

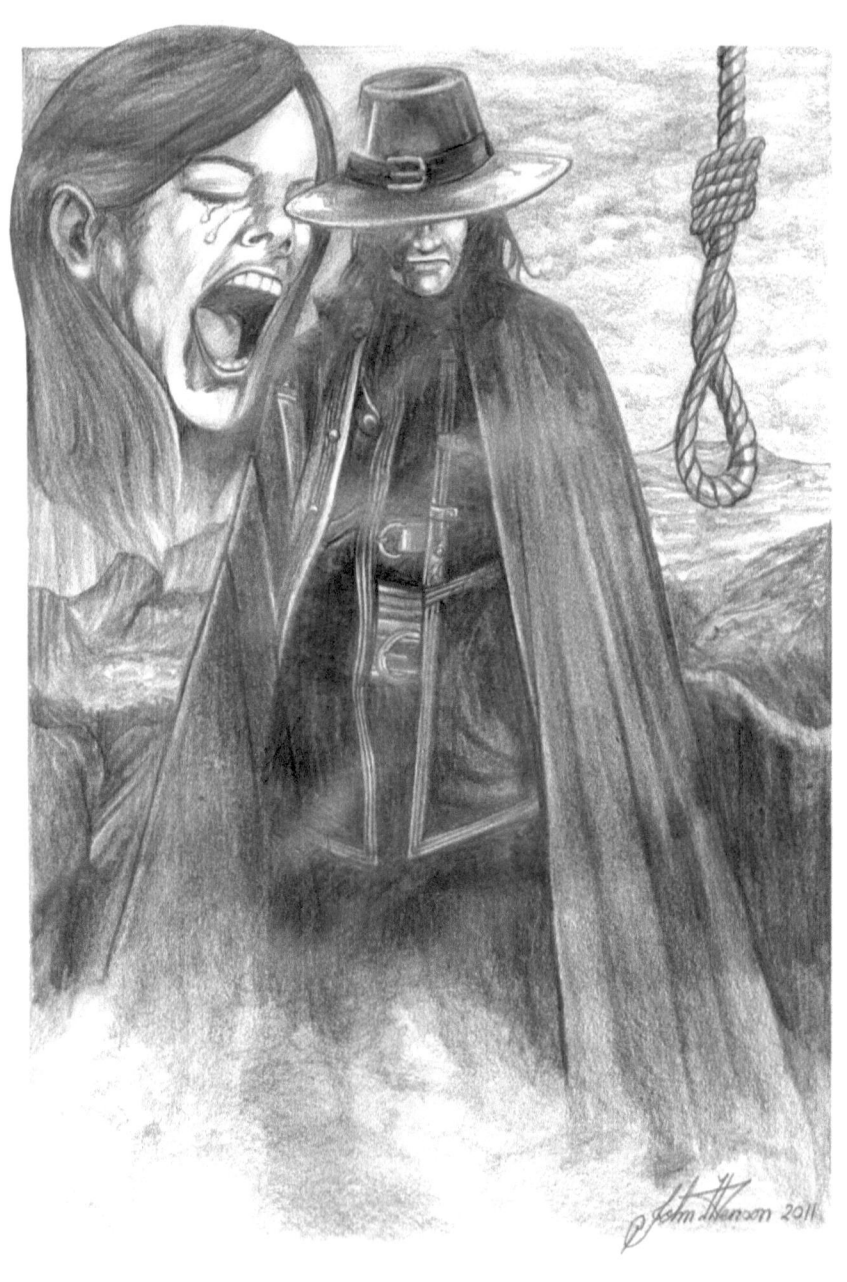

The Dark Man

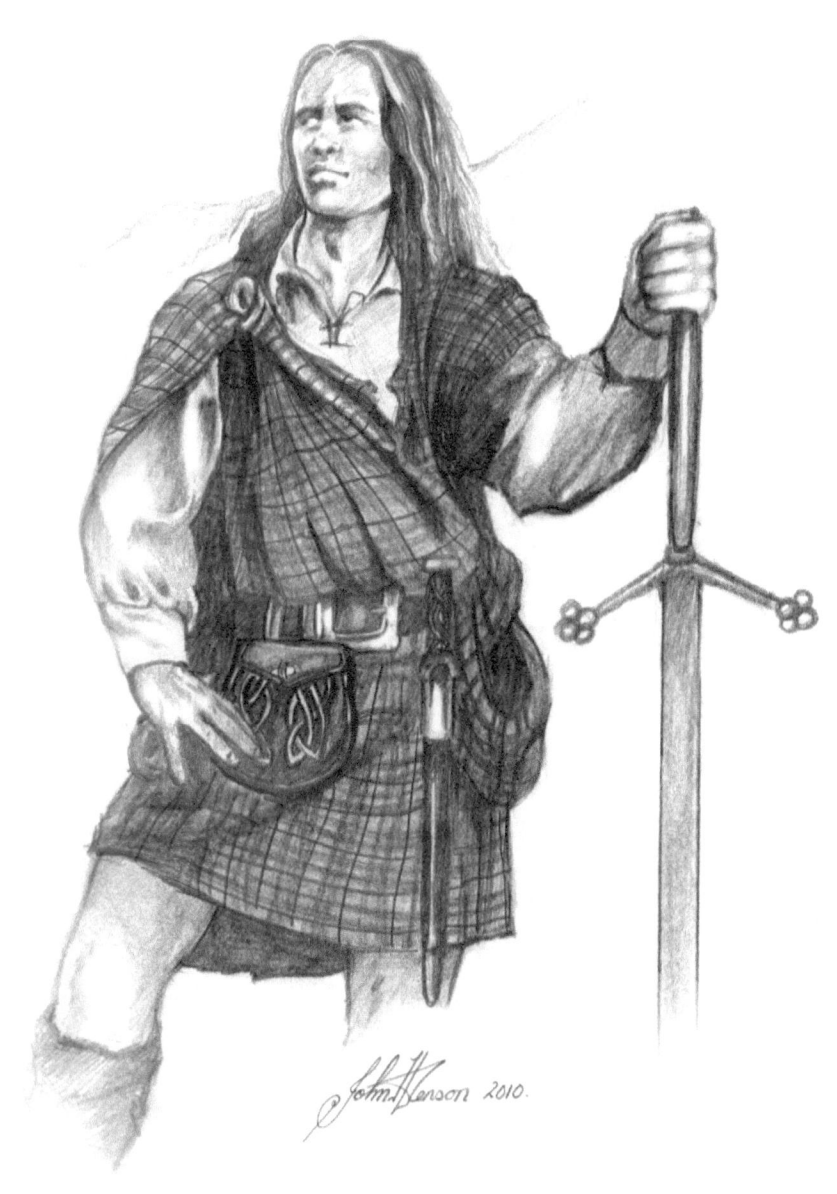

Mort Glhinne Comhaan

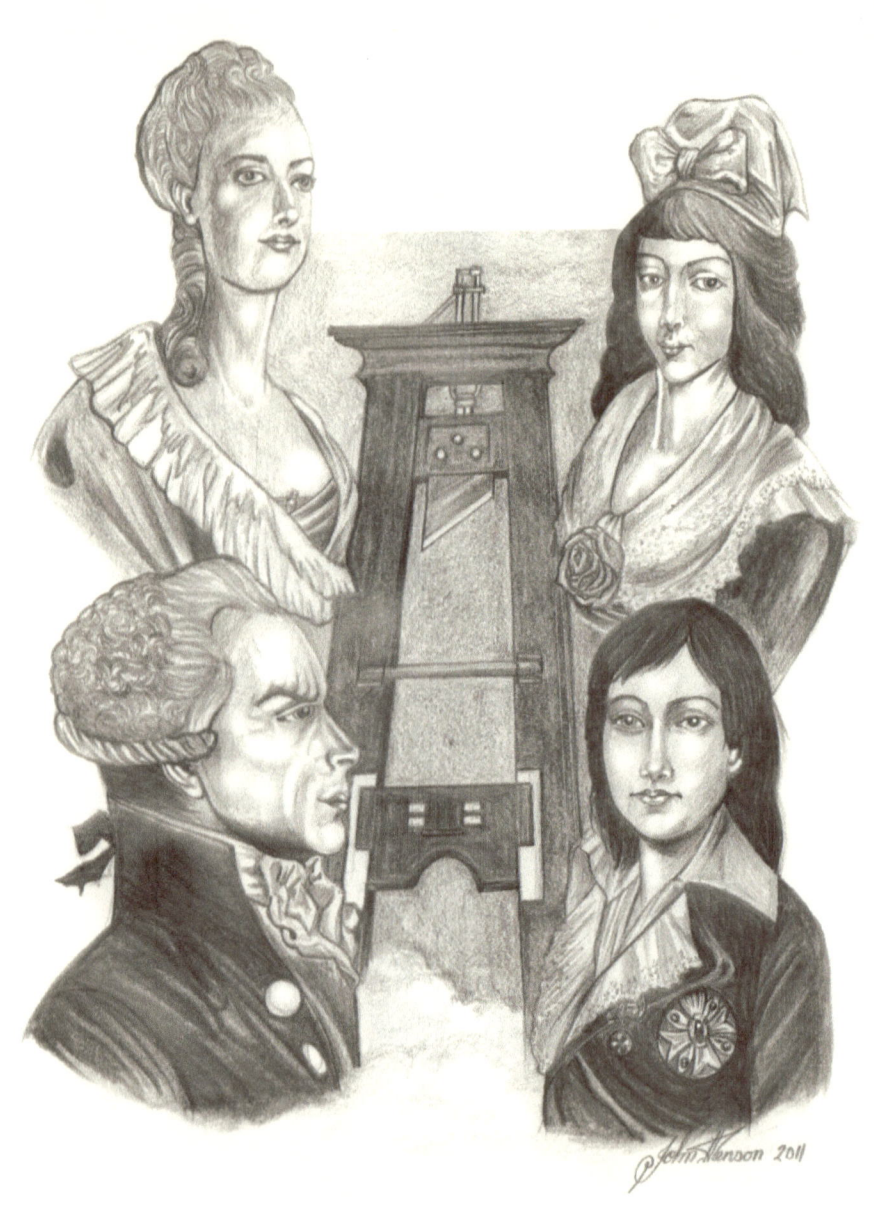

Liberte, Egalite, Fraternite

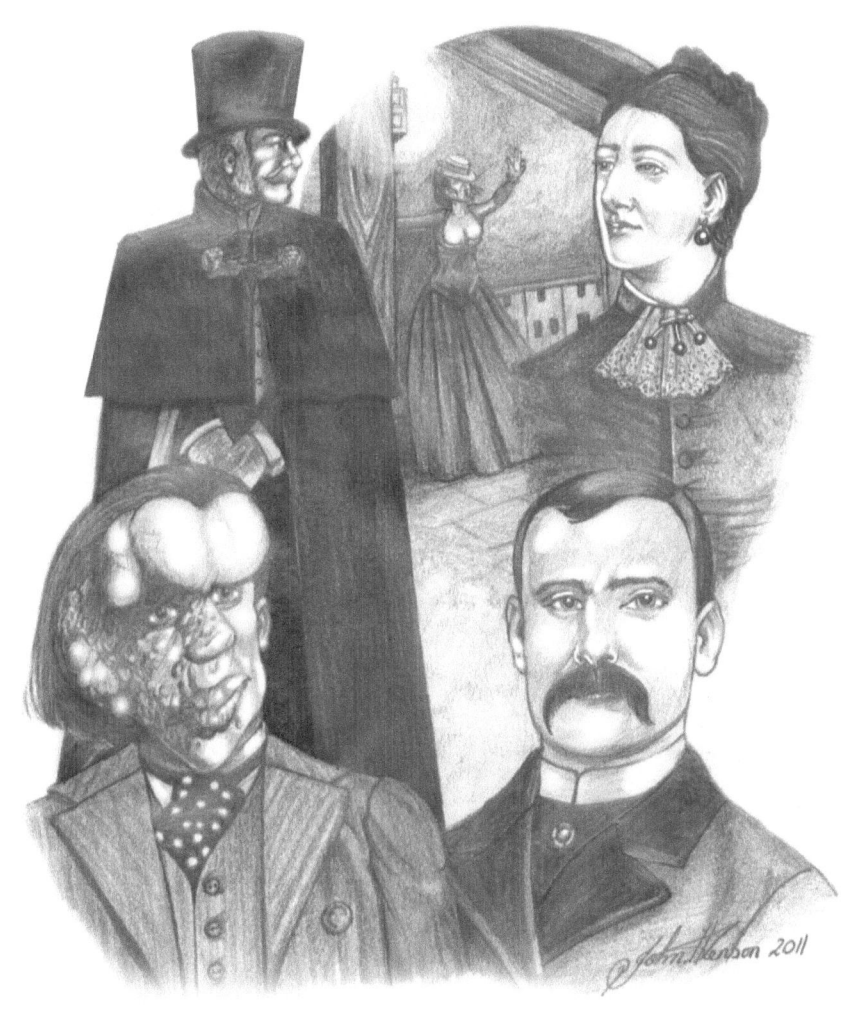

Your's Truly

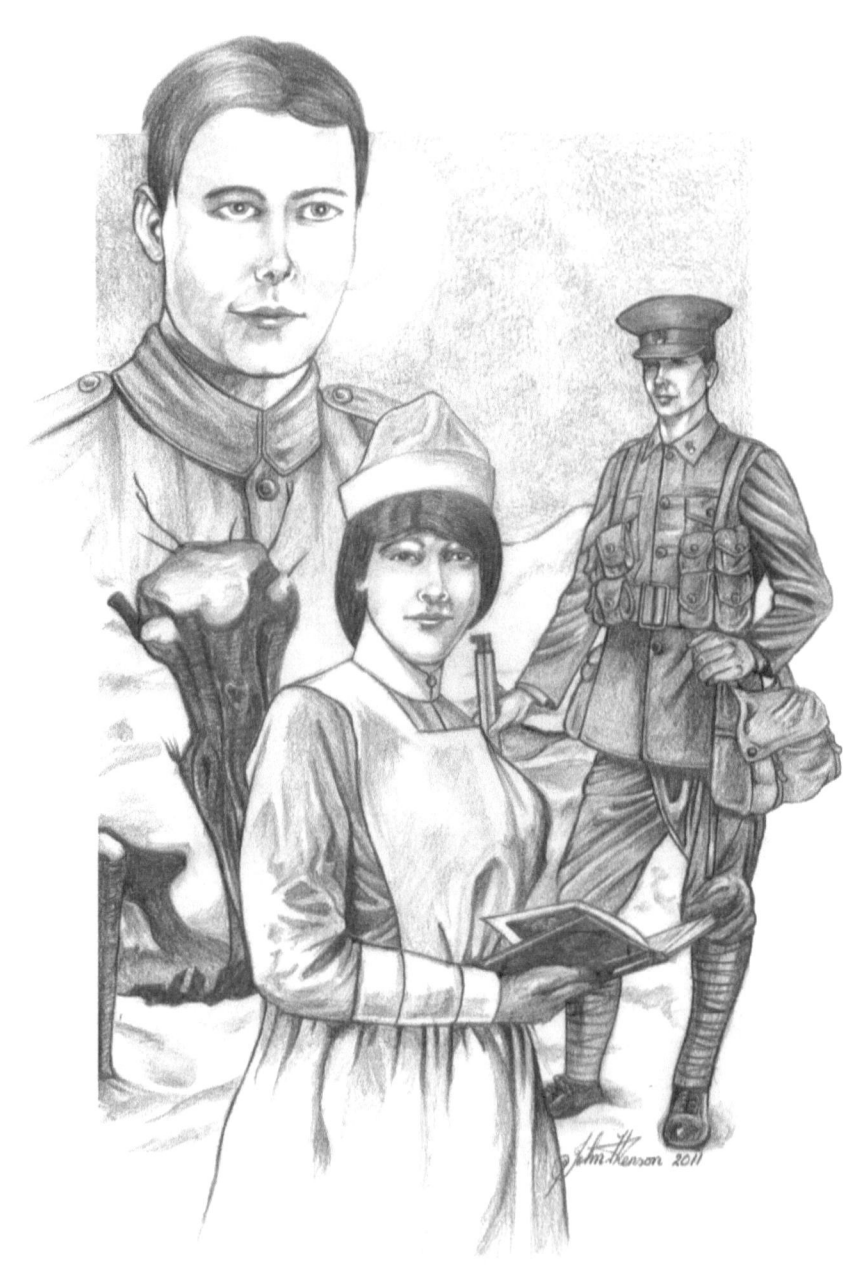

And Poppies Grew

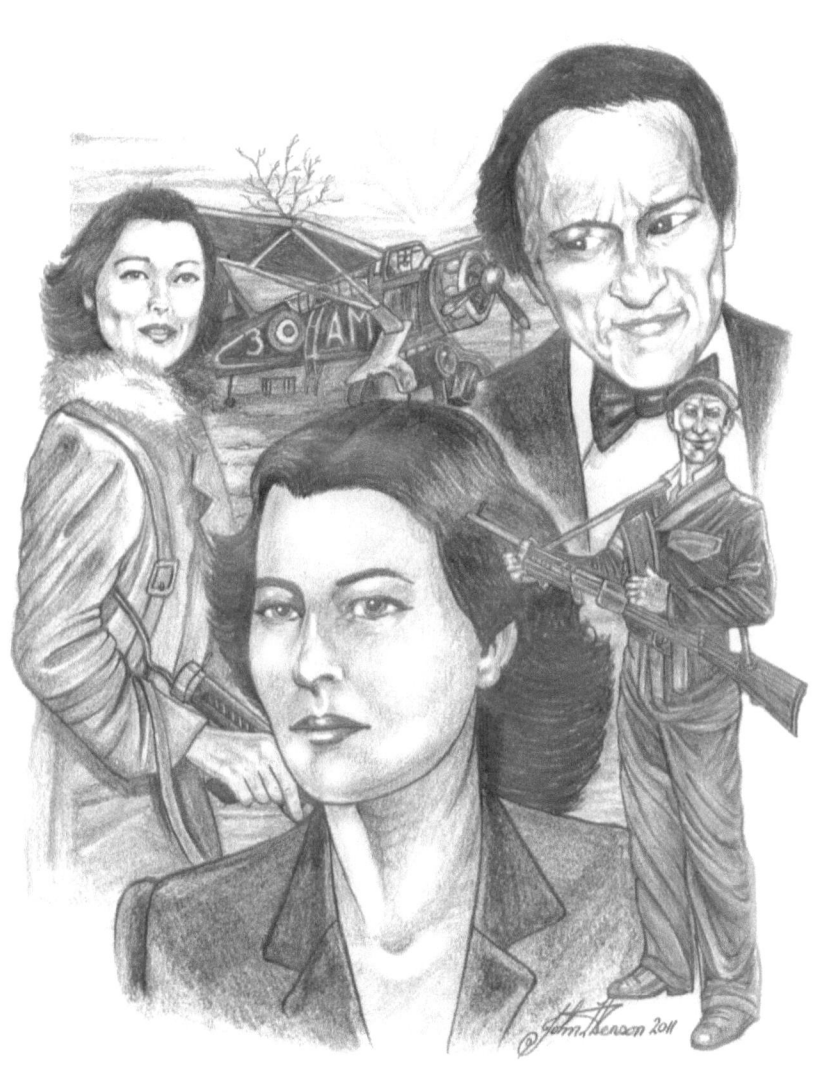

The Love That I Have

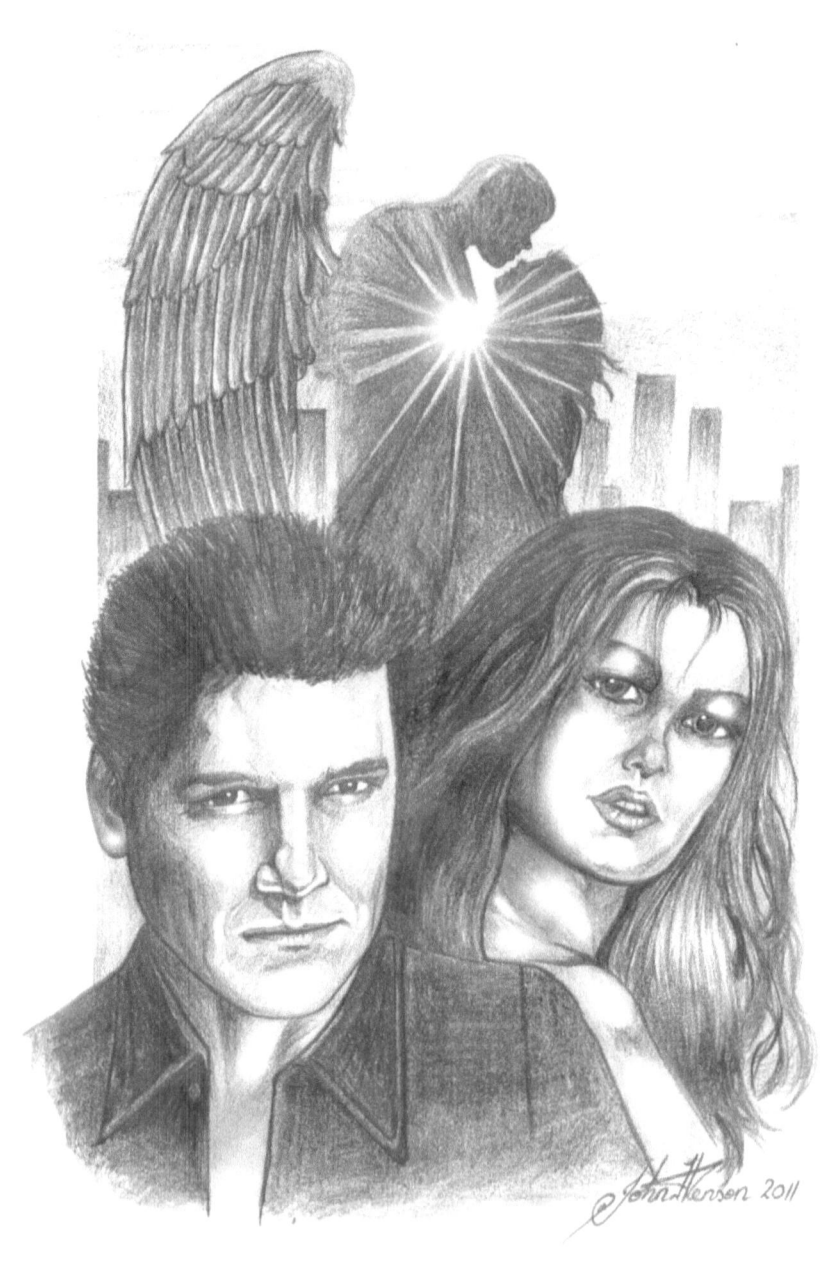

Angel of the Dawn

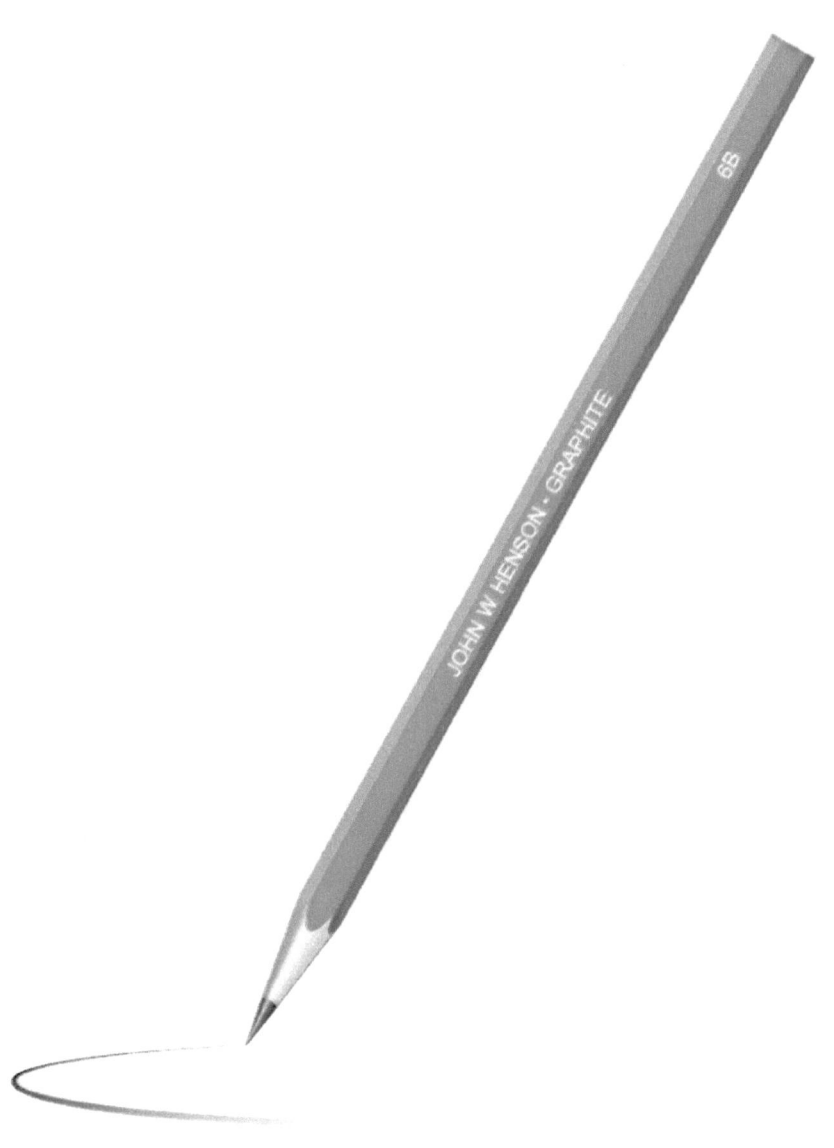

The Tale of Kathleen Laoghaire
By P F Kosak. Book illustrations

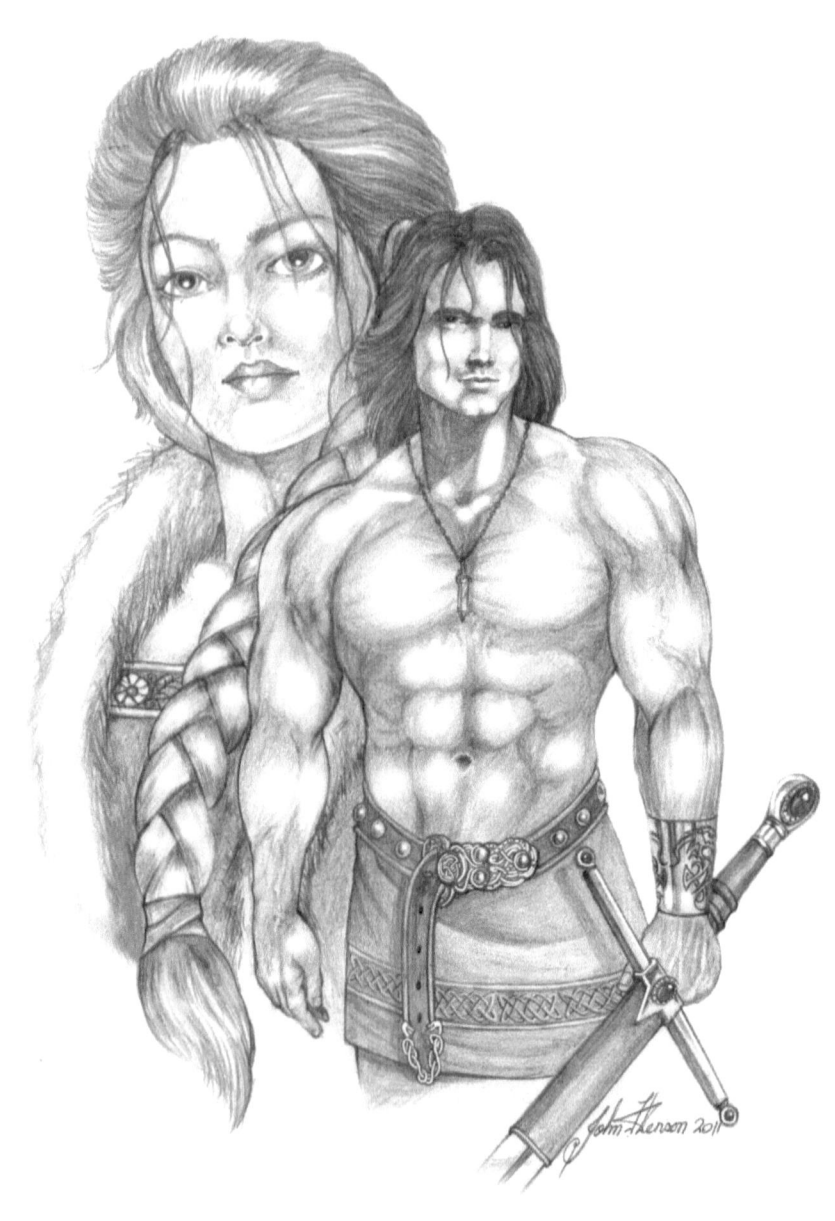

Love the Conqueror

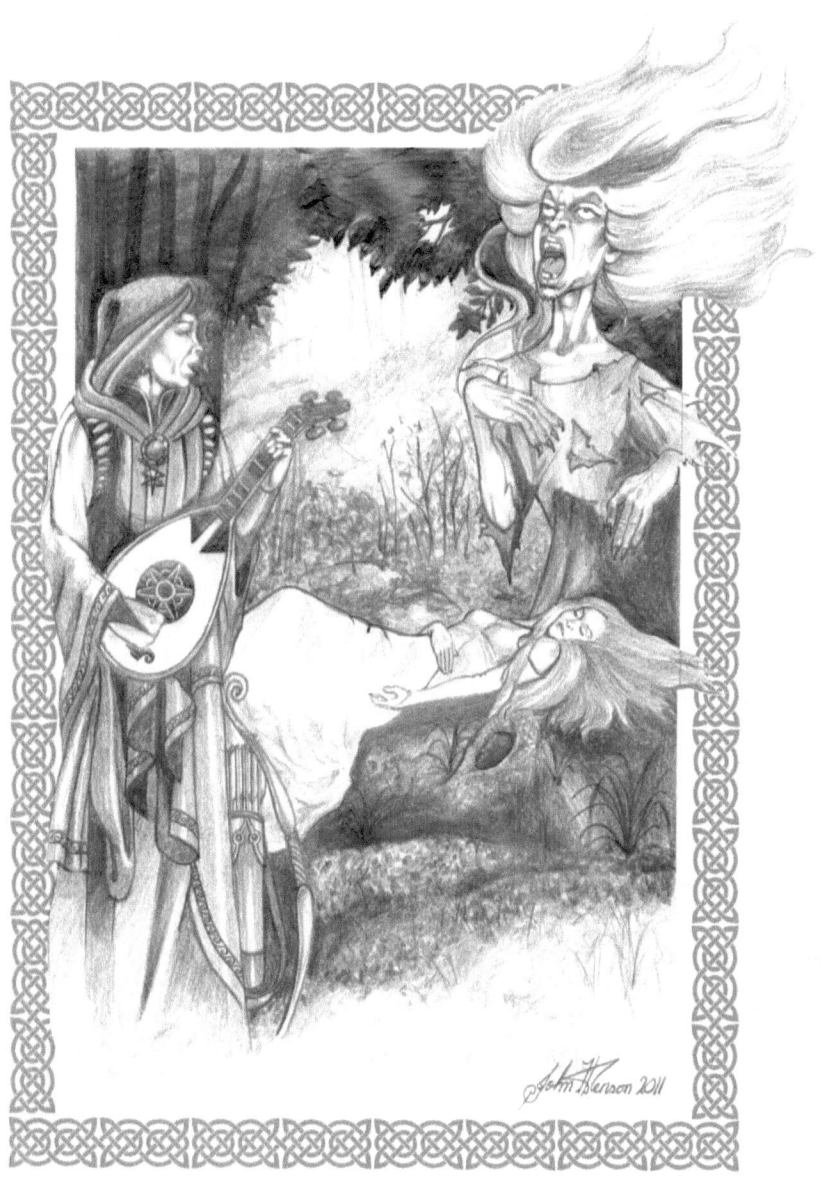

A Tale of True Love

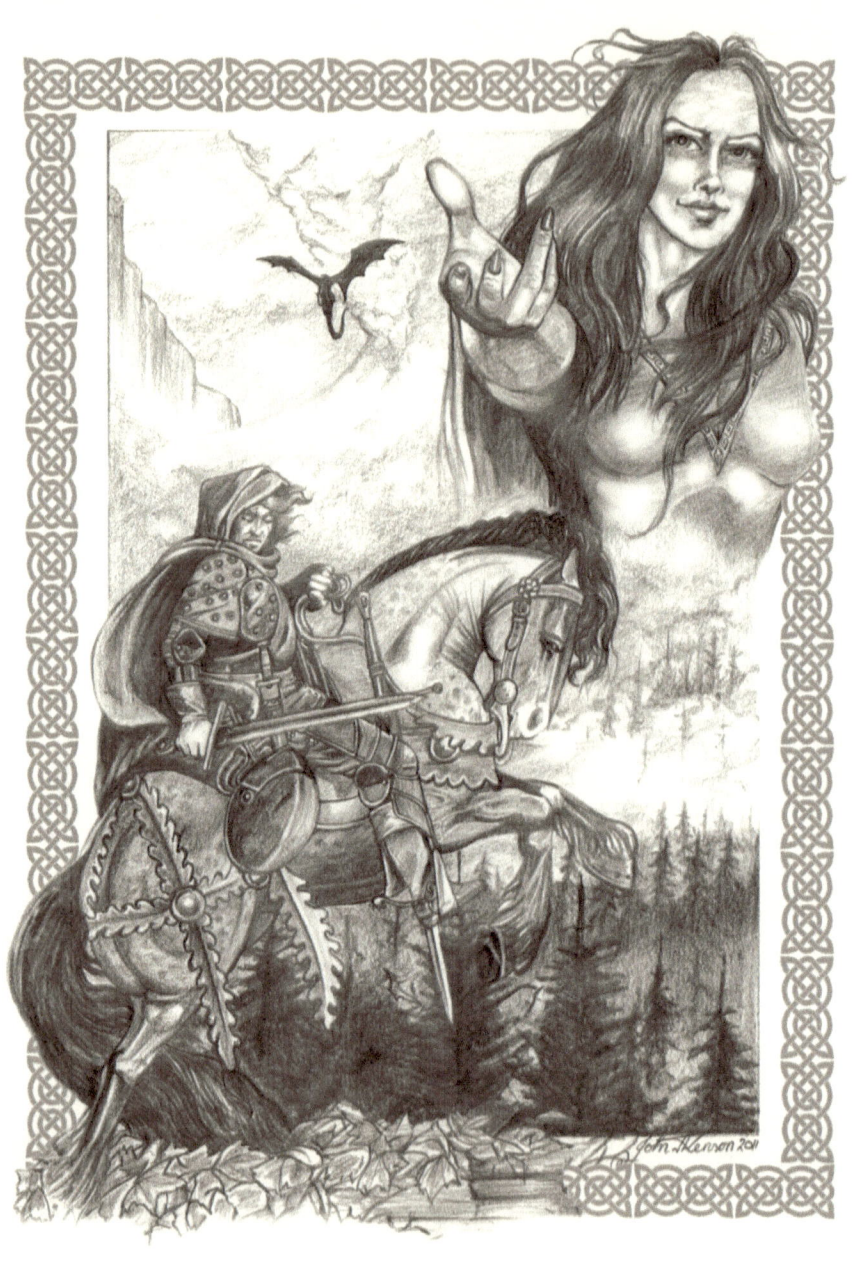

The Jealousy of a Faerie Queen

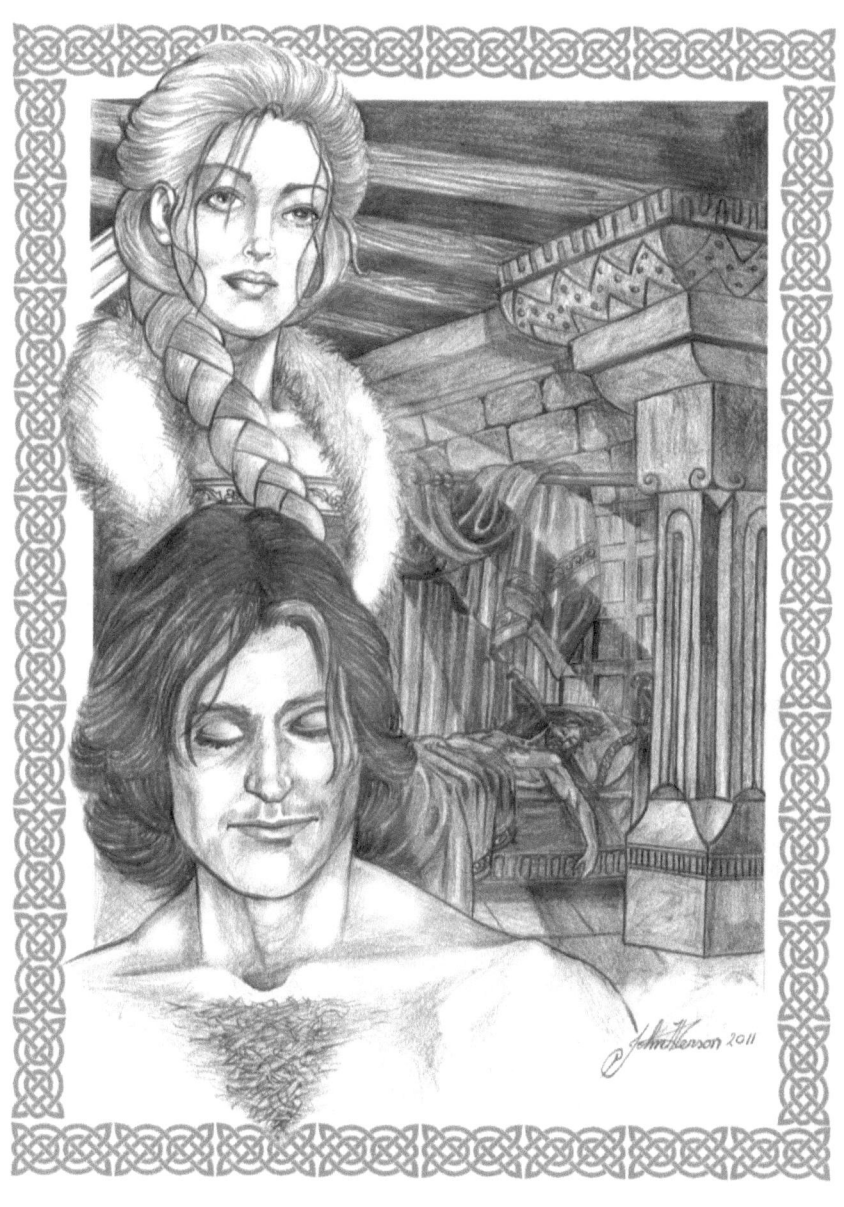

Of Faerie Queens and Knightly Things

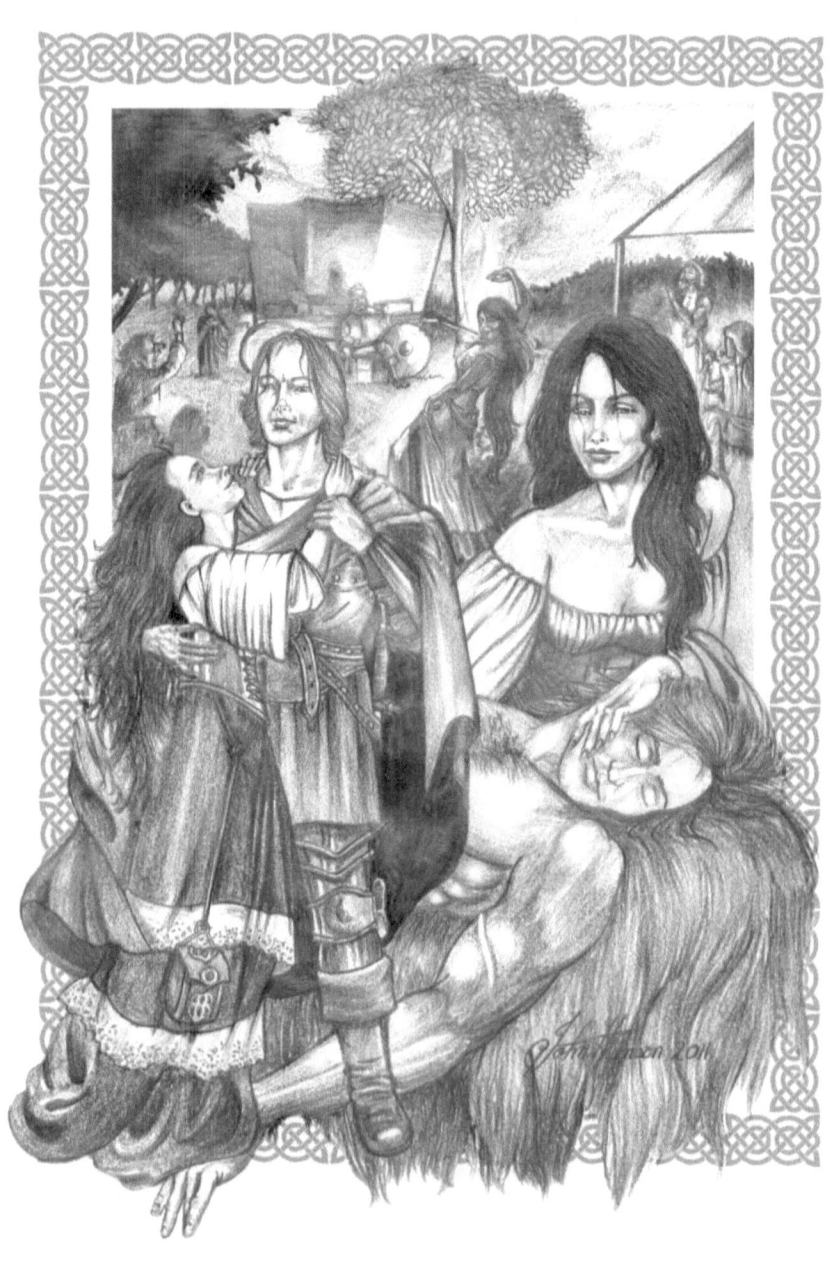

The Gypsy Camp

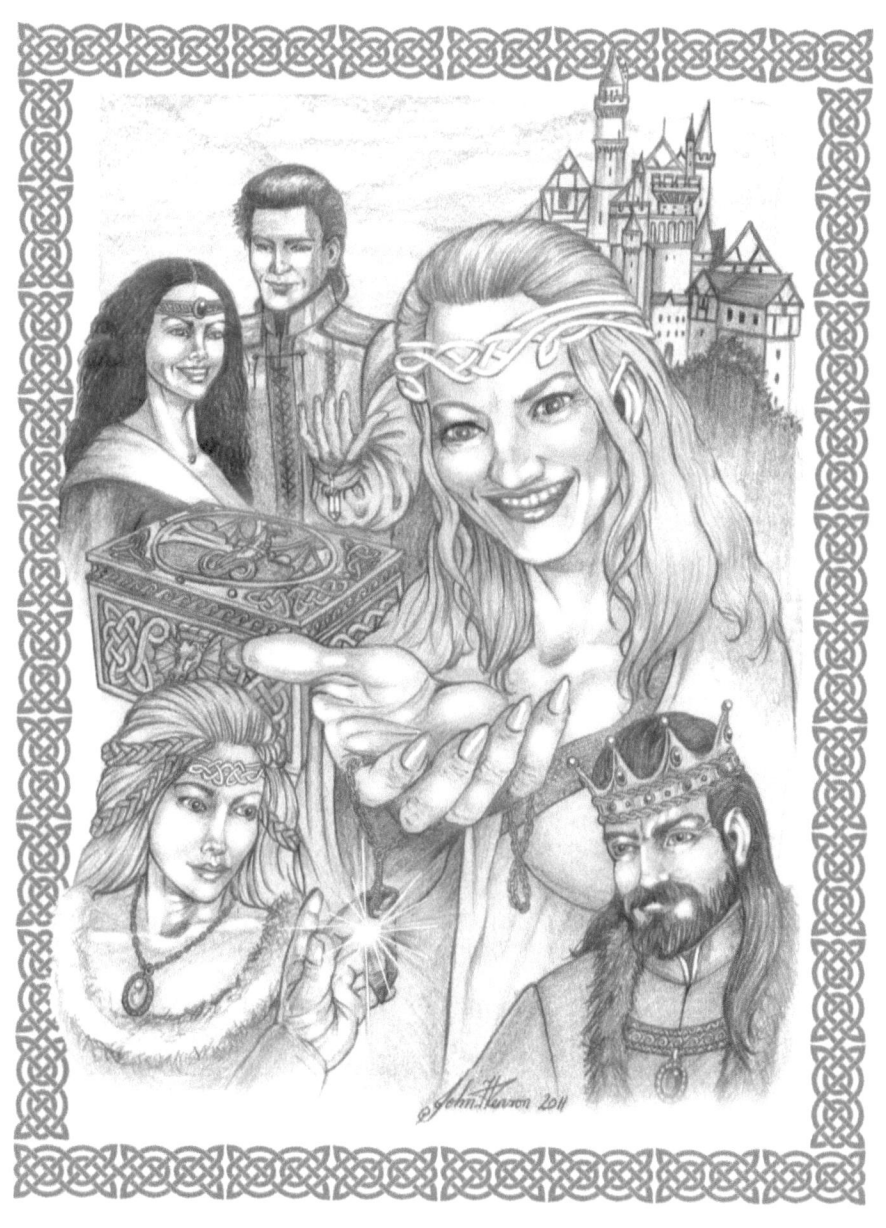

Of Amulets and Talismans

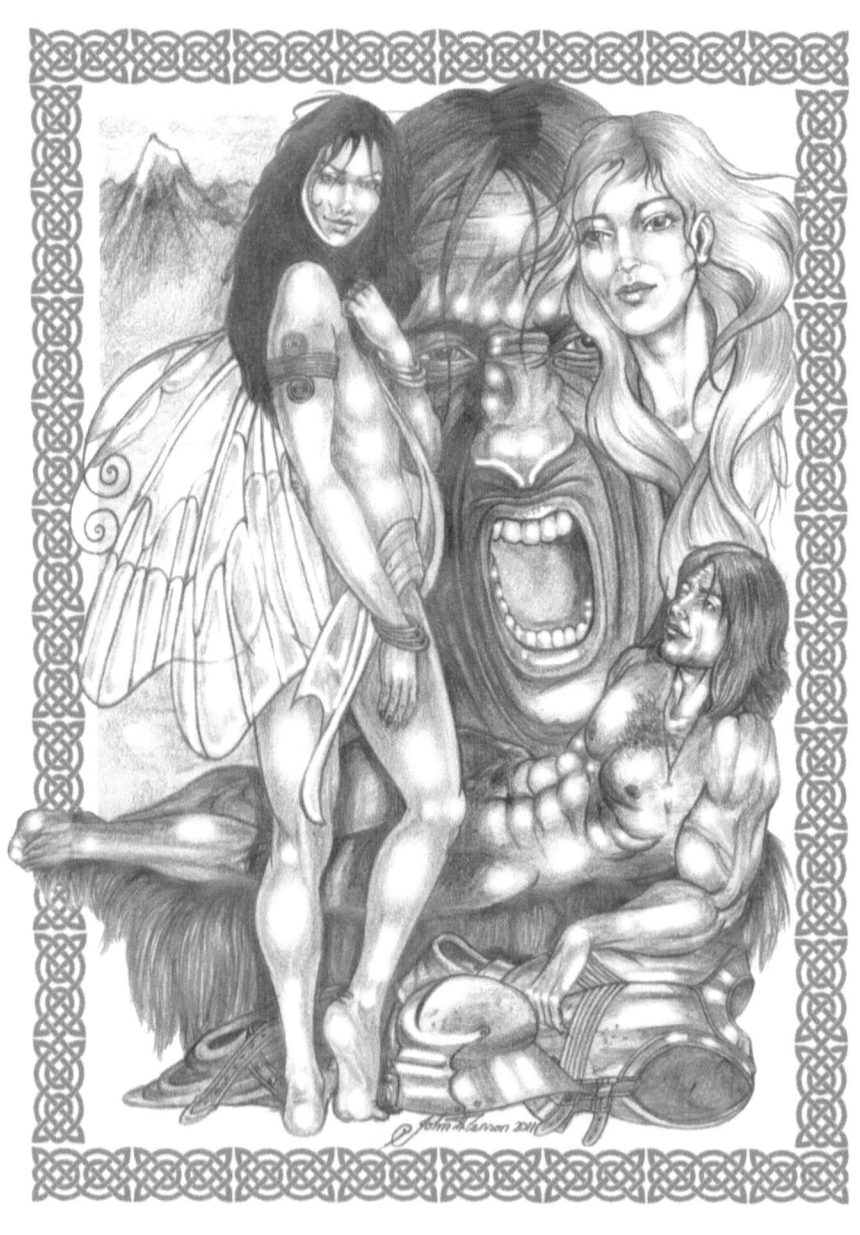

Seduction and Betrayal

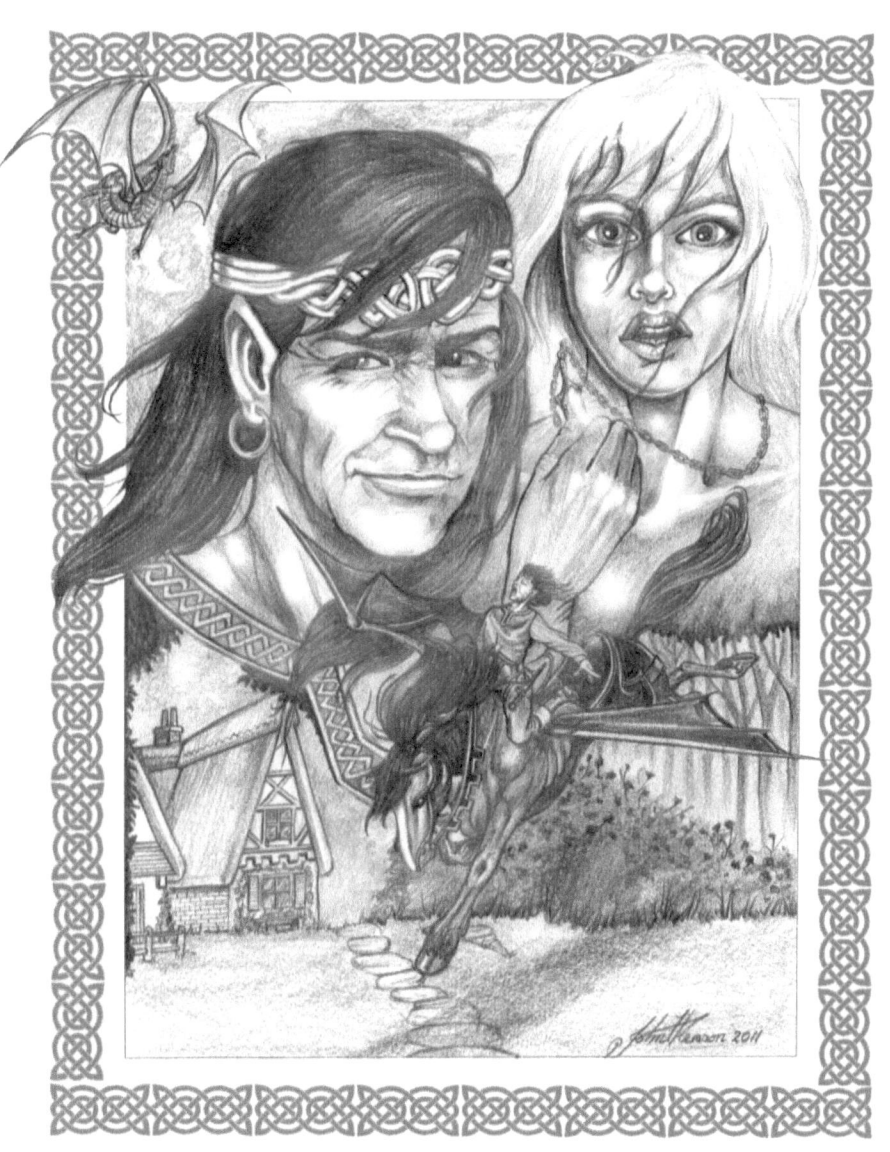

King Garamond Retaliates

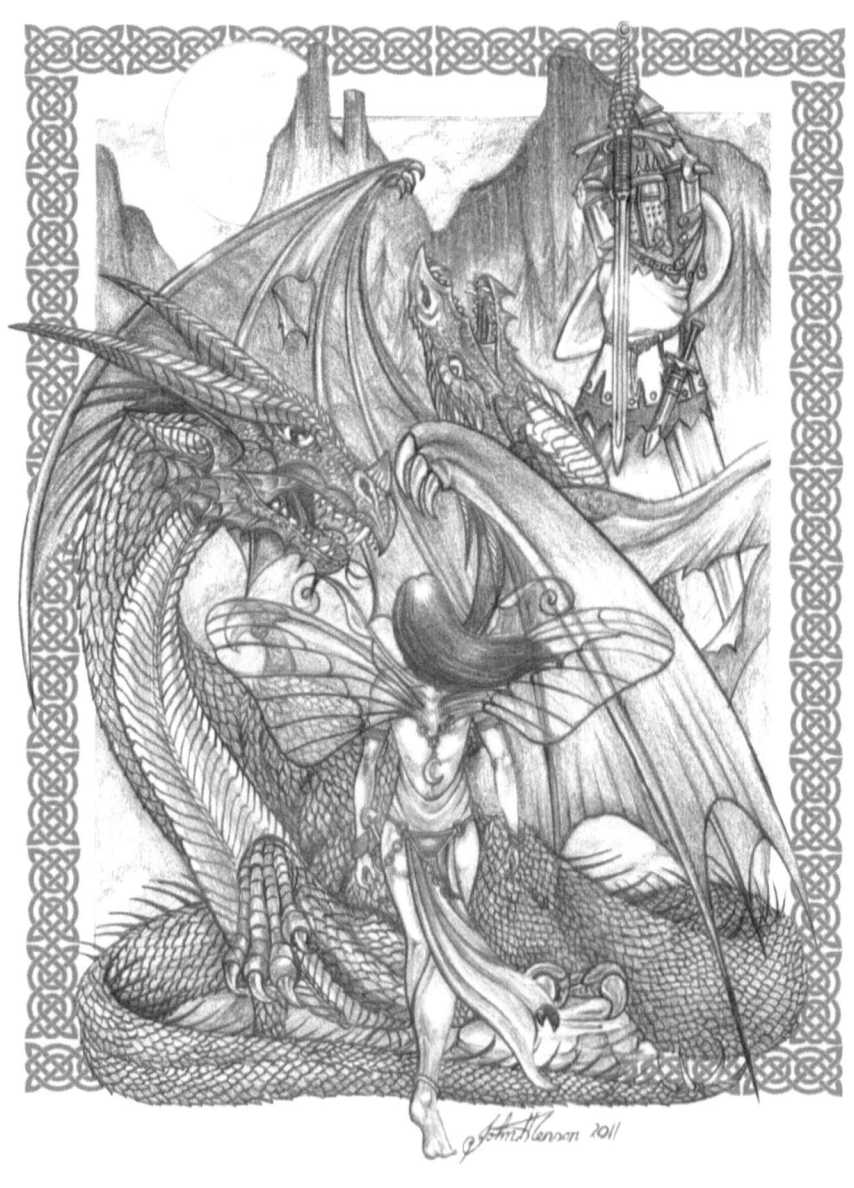

The Fury of Theron

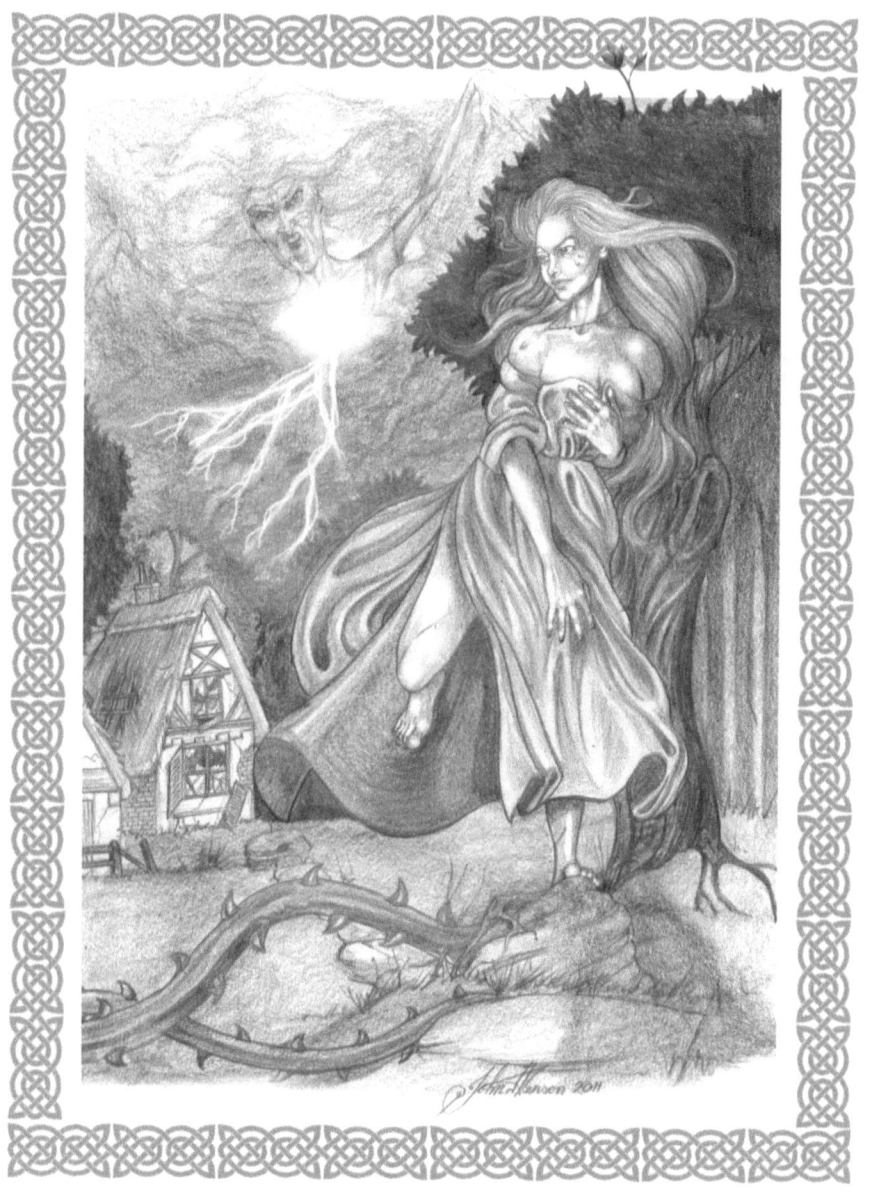

Escape

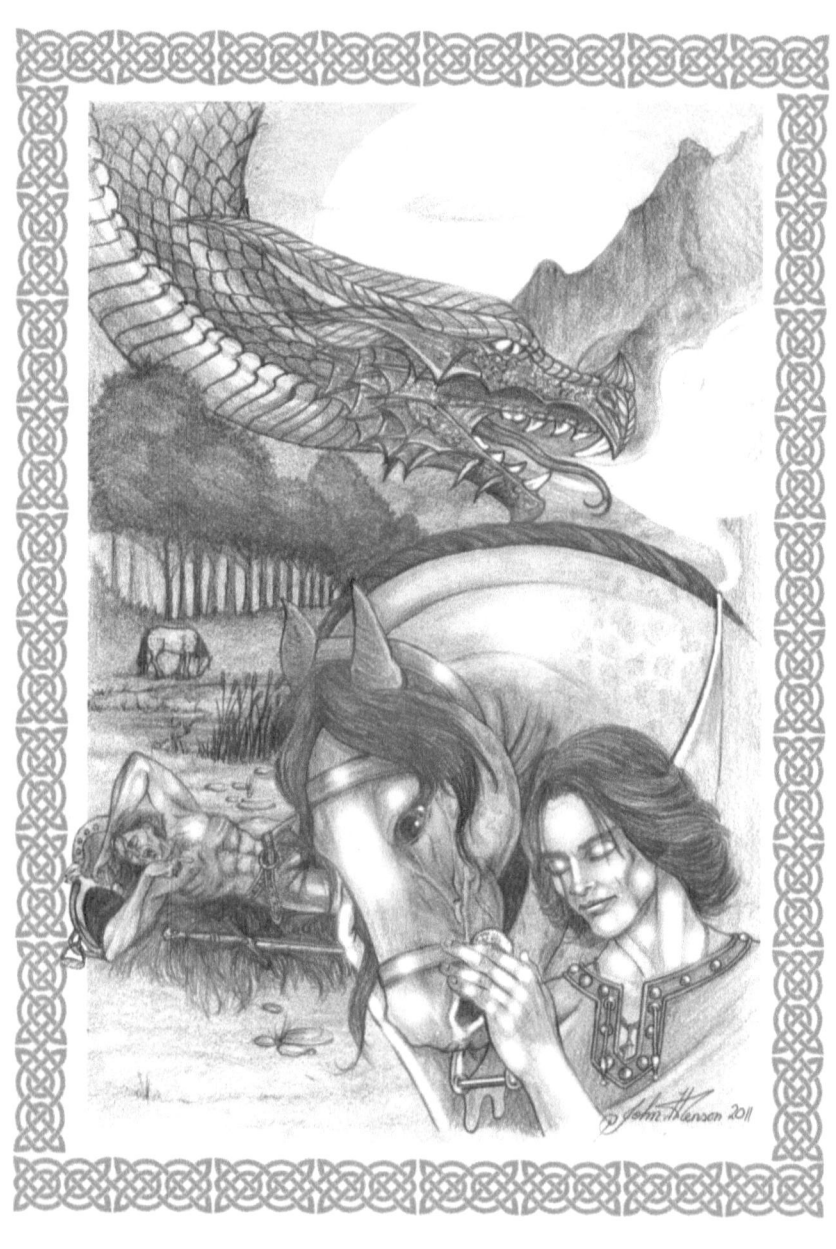

On the Eve of Battle

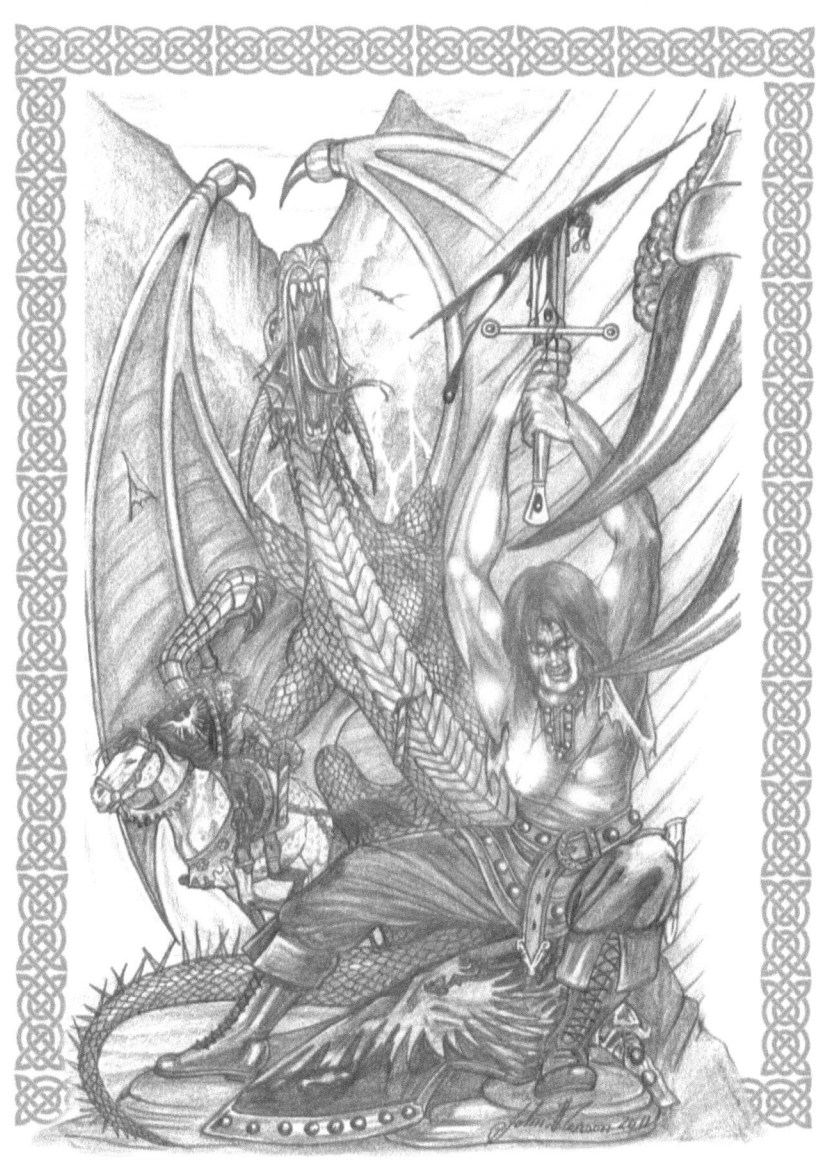

The Battle of Conall and Theron

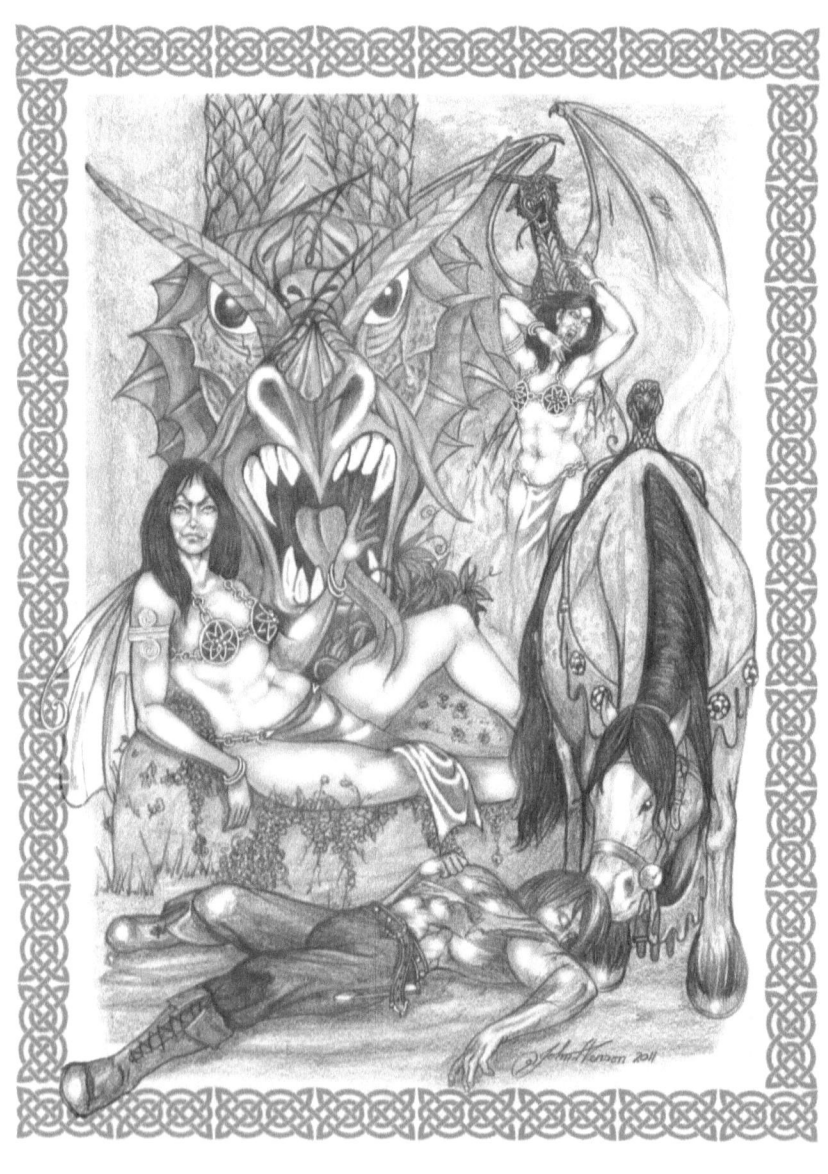

Theron's Honour Restored

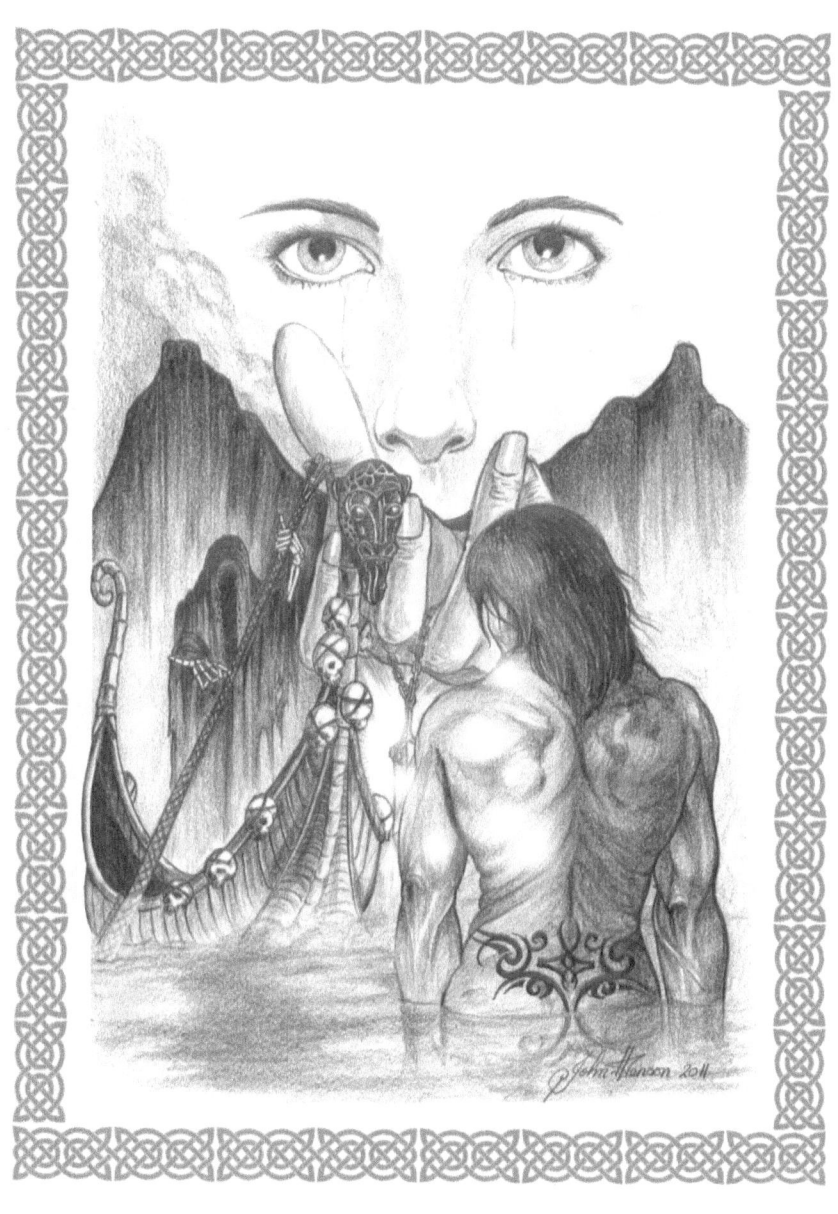

Conall's Journey

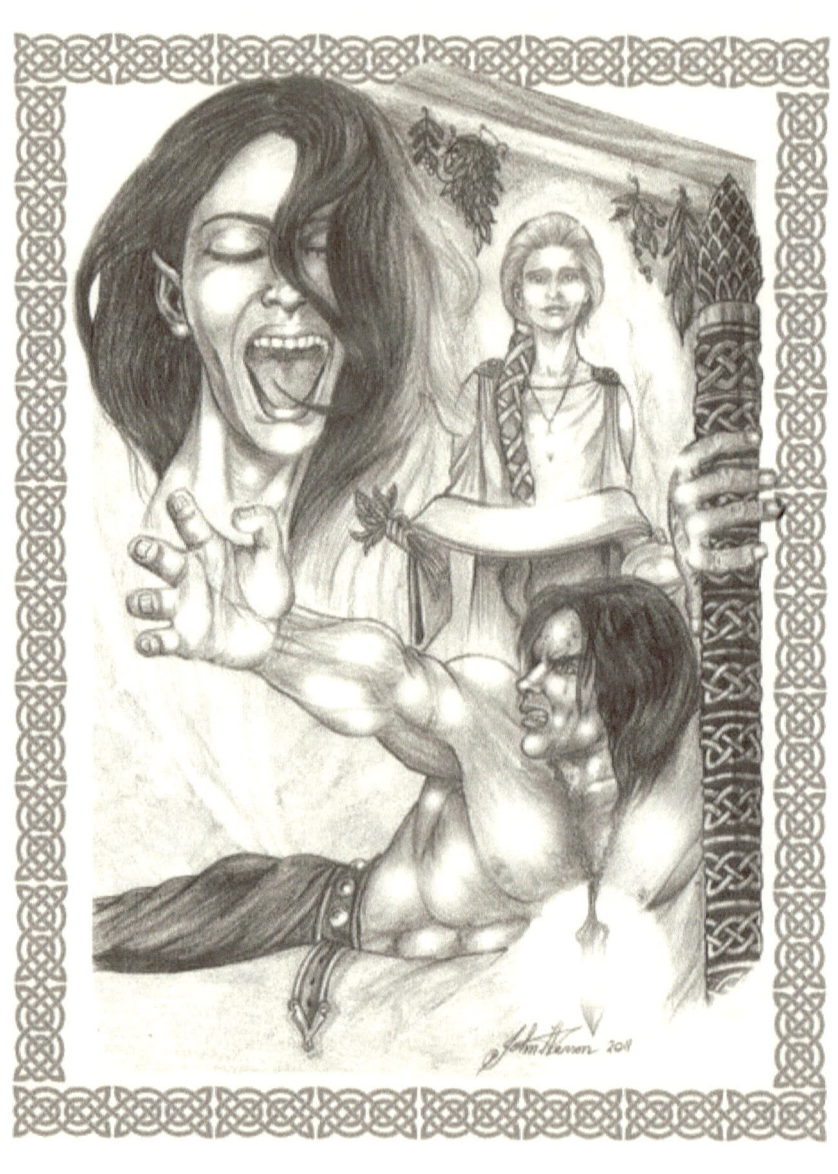

The Healing Touch

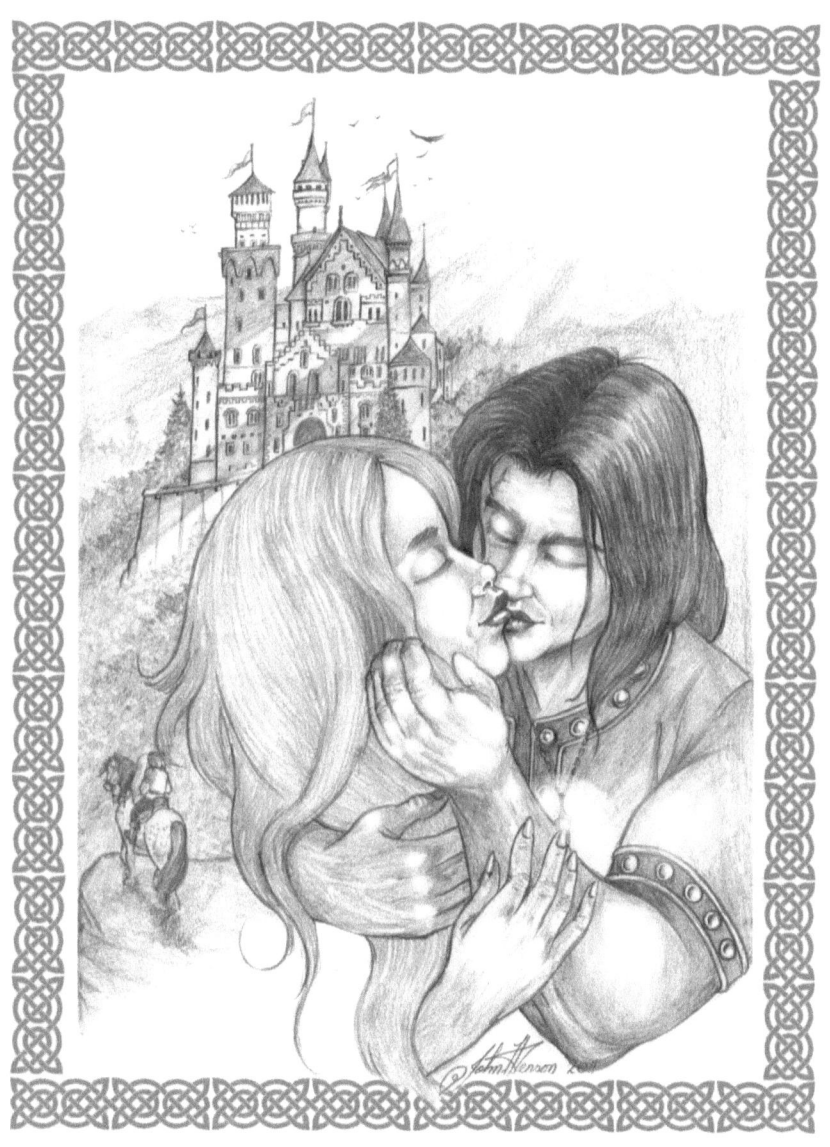

Heart and Home

Also by
John W Henson

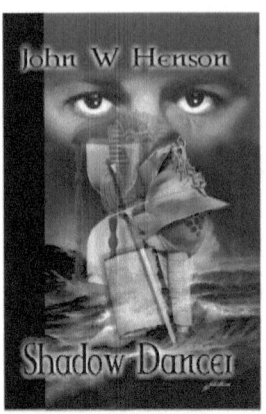

Shadow Dancer: the first collection of the poetry of John W Henson. This is the world of poetry as you have never seen it before covering diverse subjects with a fresh approach.

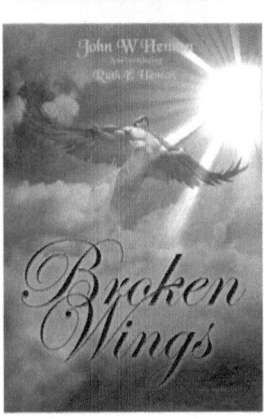

Broken Wings: *the second anthology of John W Henson's verse written with his daughter Ruth Elizabeth Henson a talented writer and artist in her own right.*

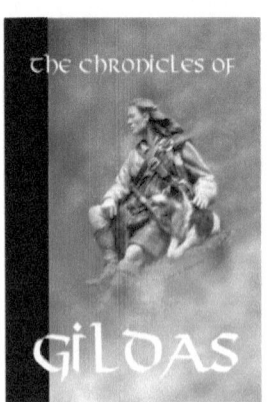

The Chronicles of Gildas

The ultimate vampyre epic. The saga of an undying love with the power to span the mists of time itself.

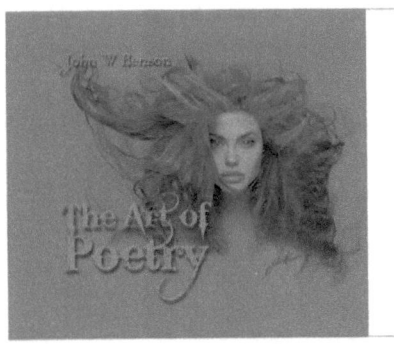

The Art of Poetry:

A portfolio of stunning illustrated verse in full colour by John W Henson. This is a book of poetry at it's very best, a real treasure and a landmark in 'The Art of Poetry'

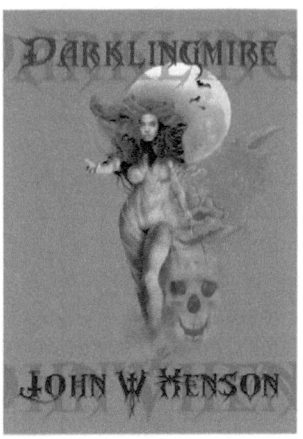

Darklingmire

a superb collection of horror poems, comical and endearing as you read of Vlad and Diptherea the vampire lovers and their rebellious daughter Pandemonium, charming and endearing they are but be warned in the second half of the book it gets serious and you may wish to leave the bedroom light on for fear of the lurkers in the shadows.

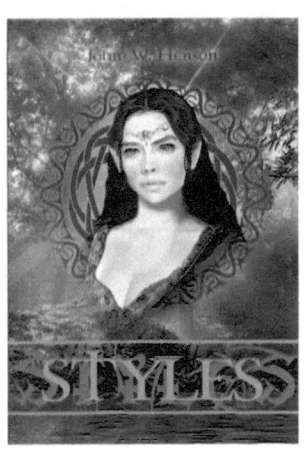

Styles: *here collected*

together for the first time the styles and shaped form poems created by John W Henson, each with full instructions and illustrated examples by the author.

You have not read poetry until you have read the works of

John W Henson

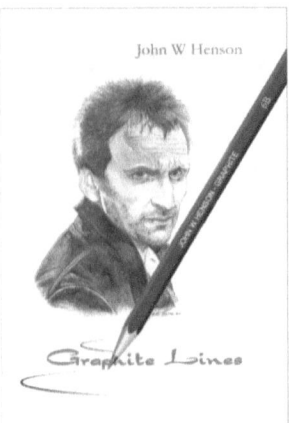

Graphite Lines: *this book is a tribute to Mr Anthony Cope Scothern. The author's art teacher. In this volume John W Henson pays tribute to the man and the school that he taught at. In verse and quality pencil illustration he shows that the patience and encouragement of a great man were not wasted.*

Poppies:

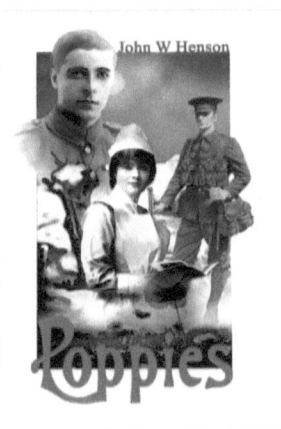

this is a celebration of heroes through the ages from the mythological heroes of the ancient Greeks through the history of warriors of all ages, the glory, honour and horror of combat and warfare. It's all here from the points of view of the people involved from the professional soldier to the ordinary people and even the voices of the children touched by war are heard in this truly moving collection of poems

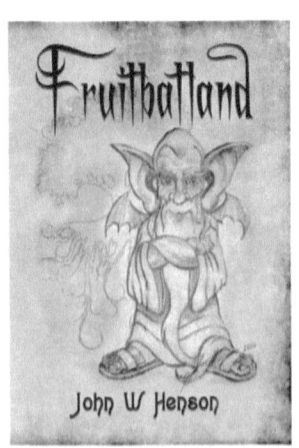

Fruitbatland: what is it? It is where all things are possible where nonsense makes complete sense, where the amusing and humble fruitbats live out their simple lives. The inhabitants of this land will touch your hearts, their aspirations, desires and problems you will all know as you feel for these endearing little folk. Populated with strange and absurd creatures you will grow to love. Where is it? why it is in the hearts of all of us.

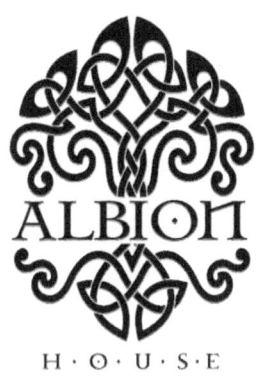

ALBION
H·O·U·S·E

Albion House Publishing

www.ingramcontent.com/pod-product-compliance
Lightning Source LLC
Chambersburg PA
CBHW022103170526
45157CB00004B/1464